Are you excited by the extraordinary? Intrigued by the incredible?

You're in the right place at the right time. Page one, *Awesome Truth.*

In a very short time, you'll know more than the next guy about Bible truths, church history, great Christians, God's creation, and astounding and unusual occurrences that just so happen to be true.

Extremely doubtful that you've been here, done this. Turn the page.

Written and illustrated
by Eddie Eddings

A Barbour Book

ISBN 1-55748-905-X

Published by Barbour and Company, Inc.
        P.O. Box 719
        Uhrichsville, OH 44683

Printed in the United States of America

To my wife, Mary, and to my children, Amy, Tammy, Jenny, and David, and their spouses, Hal, Chris, and Tahmmy.

"To know God's will is life's greatest knowledge; to do God's will is life's greatest achievement."

Here's a book that is both fun and edifying. It's a fascinating collection of rich thoughts, historical and biblical facts, and life-changing truths, laid out in a fresh and ingenious format. Eddie Eddings has a unique gift, which he uses to the glory of God. Read and enjoy.

John MacArthur

Thanks to James Kinman for his dedication and example.

Thanks to Lee Graham for his constant encouragement.

Thanks to Mike Garrett for his "pruf" reading.

Thanks to Andy Raiford, Kevin Sparkman, Bob and Mike Ross, and Eva and Don Tobola.

Thanks to my sisters, Ginger Hilton and Sandy Gray, for reading this far to see if I mentioned them, too.

AWESOME TRUTH by Eddie Eddings

"GOD IS IN THE REMNANT BUSINESS TODAY. HE ALWAYS HAS BEEN. HE IS NOT CONVERTING THE WORLD, HE IS TAKING OUT A PEOPLE FOR HIS NAME."

— VANCE HAVNER

WHO AM I?

① I AM AN OLD TESTAMENT FUGITIVE PROPHET.

② I AM EVEN MENTIONED IN THE BOOK MOBY DICK.

③ MY PRAYER CLOSET WAS MORE LIKE A SUBMARINE! (ANSWER BELOW)

IT WASN'T UNTIL THE 1800's THAT WILLIAM FERREL FORMULATED "FERREL'S LAW" WHICH EXPLAINS THE PREVAILING DIRECTIONS OF THE WINDS OVER THE EARTH... BUT GOD TELLS US **THAT** IN ECCLESIASTES CHAPTER 1 VERSE 6 WRITTEN IN 1000 B.C. !!

James Garfield, THE 20th PRESIDENT OF THE UNITED STATES, WAS ONCE A DISCIPLE OF CHRIST **EVANGELIST!**

BIBLE QUIZ

DOES THE BIBLE SAY THAT ALL MEN HAVE SAVING FAITH?

NO! 2 THESSALONIANS 3:2 EXPLICITLY STATES,"...FOR NOT ALL HAVE FAITH."

ANSWER TO "WHO AM I?" — JONAH

11

AWESOME TRUTH by Eddie Eddings

"WHAT USE IS DEEPER KNOWLEDGE IF WE HAVE SHALLOWER HEARTS?"

LEONARD RAVENHILL

WHO AM I?

① I WAS BORN IN SCOTLAND IN 1902 AND ORDAINED TO THE PRESBYTERIAN MINISTRY IN 1931.

② I WAS THE CHAPLAIN TO THE U.S. SENATE FROM 1947-1949, WHERE I WAS KNOWN FOR REMARKABLY PITHY PRAYERS.

③ I WROTE "MR. JONES, MEET THE MASTER."

(ANSWER BELOW)

THE PILGRIMS HAD PLANNED ON COMING TO AMERICA IN TWO SHIPS, THE MAYFLOWER AND THE SPEEDWELL BUT THE SPEEDWELL DID NOT QUALIFY AS SEAWORTHY.

IN WASHINGTON, D.C. NO BUILDING CAN BE CONSTRUCTED TALLER THAN THE CAPITOL!

BIBLE QUIZ:

WHAT LANGUAGES WERE USED IN THE SIGN OVER THE CROSS OF CHRIST?

HEBREW, GREEK, and LATIN (JOHN 19:20)

ANSWER TO "WHO AM I?" ———— PETER MARSHALL

AWESOME TRUTH by Eddie Eddings

"GOD WAS THE MASTER OF CEREMONIES AT THE CROSS."

ERNEST REISINGER

WHO AM I?

① AS A YOUNG MAN I ESCAPED FROM THE PARIS POLICE BY CLIMBING DOWN A ROPE MADE OUT OF BEDCLOTHES THROUGH THE BACK WINDOW OF MY APARTMENT.

② A SEARCH COMMITTEE TRIED TO HELP ME FIND A WIFE.

③ I COMPLETED THE FIRST EDITION OF "THE INSTITUTES OF THE CHRISTIAN RELIGION" WHEN I WAS 26 YEARS OLD.

(ANSWER BELOW)

THOSE WHO FIND THEMSELVES IN HEAVEN HAVE ONLY GOD TO THANK, WHEREAS THOSE WHO FIND THEMSELVES UNDER JUDGMENT HAVE ONLY THEMSELVES TO BLAME.

A NEWBORN **PANDA** IS SMALLER THAN A MOUSE!

BIBLE QUIZ: WHAT WOMAN WORE THE FIRST BRIDAL VEIL MENTIONED IN THE BIBLE?

REBEKAH (GENESIS 24:65)

"THE FEAR OF THE LORD IS TO HATE EVIL."

PROVERBS 8:13

ANSWER TO "WHO AM I?" — JOHN CALVIN

13

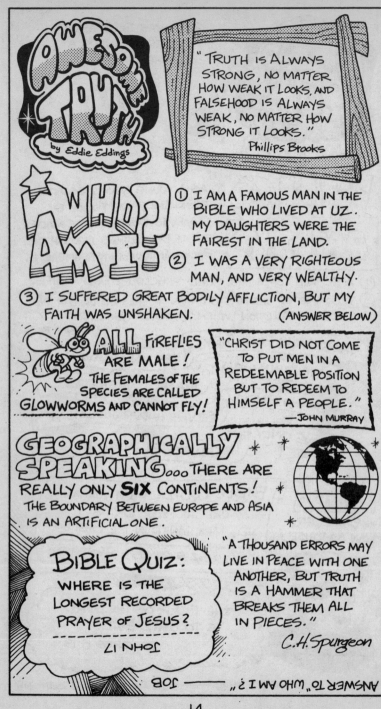

AWESOME TRUTH by Eddie Eddings

"TRUTH IS ALWAYS STRONG, NO MATTER HOW WEAK IT LOOKS, AND FALSEHOOD IS ALWAYS WEAK, NO MATTER HOW STRONG IT LOOKS."
Phillips Brooks

WHO AM I?

① I AM A FAMOUS MAN IN THE BIBLE WHO LIVED AT UZ. MY DAUGHTERS WERE THE FAIREST IN THE LAND.

② I WAS A VERY RIGHTEOUS MAN, AND VERY WEALTHY.

③ I SUFFERED GREAT BODILY AFFLICTION, BUT MY FAITH WAS UNSHAKEN. (ANSWER BELOW)

ALL FIREFLIES ARE MALE! THE FEMALES OF THE SPECIES ARE CALLED GLOWWORMS AND CANNOT FLY!

"CHRIST DID NOT COME TO PUT MEN IN A REDEEMABLE POSITION BUT TO REDEEM TO HIMSELF A PEOPLE."
—JOHN MURRAY

GEOGRAPHICALLY SPEAKING...THERE ARE REALLY ONLY **SIX** CONTINENTS! THE BOUNDARY BETWEEN EUROPE AND ASIA IS AN ARTIFICIAL ONE.

BIBLE QUIZ: WHERE IS THE LONGEST RECORDED PRAYER OF JESUS?
- - - - - - - - - -
JOHN 17

"A THOUSAND ERRORS MAY LIVE IN PEACE WITH ONE ANOTHER, BUT TRUTH IS A HAMMER THAT BREAKS THEM ALL IN PIECES."
C.H. Spurgeon

ANSWER TO "WHO AM I?" —— JOB

14

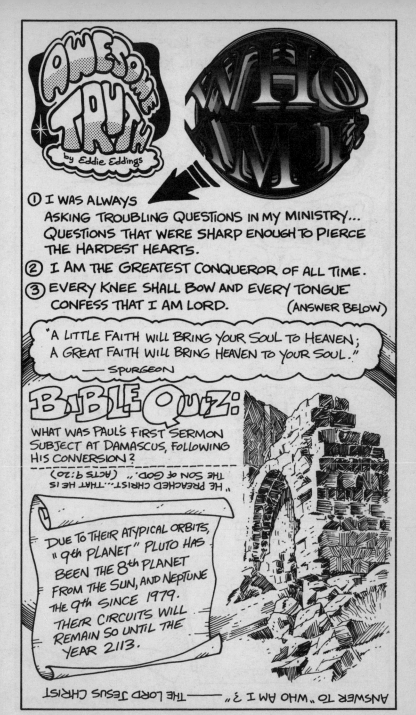

AWESOME TRUTH by Eddie Eddings

WHO AM I

① I WAS ALWAYS ASKING TROUBLING QUESTIONS IN MY MINISTRY... QUESTIONS THAT WERE SHARP ENOUGH TO PIERCE THE HARDEST HEARTS.

② I AM THE GREATEST CONQUEROR OF ALL TIME.

③ EVERY KNEE SHALL BOW AND EVERY TONGUE CONFESS THAT I AM LORD. (ANSWER BELOW)

"A LITTLE FAITH WILL BRING YOUR SOUL TO HEAVEN; A GREAT FAITH WILL BRING HEAVEN TO YOUR SOUL."
— SPURGEON

BIBLE QUIZ:

WHAT WAS PAUL'S FIRST SERMON SUBJECT AT DAMASCUS, FOLLOWING HIS CONVERSION?

"HE PREACHED CHRIST...THAT HE IS THE SON of GOD." (ACTS 9:20)

DUE TO THEIR ATYPICAL ORBITS, "9th PLANET" PLUTO HAS BEEN THE 8th PLANET FROM THE SUN, AND NEPTUNE THE 9th SINCE 1979. THEIR CIRCUITS WILL REMAIN SO UNTIL THE YEAR 2113.

ANSWER TO "WHO AM I?" ——— THE LORD JESUS CHRIST

15

AWESOME TRUTH
by Eddie Eddings

"BY PERSEVERENCE THE SNAIL REACHED THE ARK."
C.H. SPURGEON

WHO AM I?

① MY VIEWS THAT THE CHURCH AND STATE MUST BE SEPARATE AND THAT THE STATE MUST NOT COERCE THE CONSCIENCE OF THE INDIVIDUAL ARE A TREASURED PART OF THE BAPTIST HERITAGE IN AMERICA.

② I WAS INSTRUMENTAL IN FOUNDING THE FIRST BAPTIST CHURCH IN AMERICA IN 1639.

③ I AM THE PURITAN KNOWN FOR THE FOUNDING OF RHODE ISLAND.

(ANSWER BELOW)

BIBLE QUIZ:

WHO INSTIGATED MOB ACTION AGAINST PAUL AT EPHESUS?

— DEMETRIUS — (ACTS 19)

GILBERT STUART'S PORTRAIT OF GEORGE WASHINGTON IS THE **ONLY** OBJECT TO HAVE ALWAYS BEEN IN THE WHITE HOUSE.

URGENT!

"THEOLOGY IS TO EVANGELISM, WHAT THE SKELETON IS TO THE BODY."
C.E. AUTREY

"LIFE IS TOO SHORT TO BE SMALL."
BENJAMIN DISRAELI

ANSWER TO "WHO AM I, ?" — ROGER WILLIAMS

AWESOME TRUTH
by Eddie Eddings

"LOVE IS NOT BLIND. LUST IS BLIND. IF LOVE IS BLIND, GOD IS BLIND."
— GORDON PALMER

WHO AM I?

① MY ARMY WAS HAND-PICKED BY ME. THEY HAD TO BE GODLY, HONEST MEN WHO EMBRACED A CALVINISTIC VIEWPOINT.

② I BECAME ONE OF THE GREAT CAVALRY LEADERS OF HISTORY AND WAS MADE LORD PROTECTOR IN 1653.

③ I REFUSED THE TITLE OF KING, WAS BURIED IN WESTMINSTER ABBEY, BUT WAS DISINTERRED IN 1661.

(ANSWER BELOW)

TRUE OR FALSE?

IN THE BOOK OF ACTS, WHICH RECORDS THE EVANGELISTIC MESSAGES and LABORS OF THE APOSTLES, GOD'S LOVE IS NEVER REFERRED TO AT ALL!

ANSWER: TRUE

MOZART WROTE A SYMPHONY WHEN HE WAS **8** YEARS OLD!

ENGLISH IS THE ONLY

LANGUAGE THAT CAPITALIZES "I", THE FIRST PERSON SINGULAR.

THE JEWISH OLD TESTAMENT COMBINES EZRA AND NEHEMIAH, AND ALL 12 MINOR PROPHETS ARE IN ONE BOOK.

BIBLE QUIZ: WHO SHUT THE DOOR OF NOAH'S ARK?

GOD (GENESIS 7:24)

ANSWER TO "WHO AM I?" — OLIVER CROMWELL

18

AWESOME TRUTH by Eddie Eddings

"A LIBERAL IS ONE WHO TRANSFORMS BIBLICAL TERMS INTO THEOLOGICAL BUBBLE GUM." ANON.

WHO AM I?

① I HAD NOT EVEN SEEN A BIBLE UNTIL I WAS TWENTY YEARS OLD.

② I MARRIED A FORMER NUN.

③ ON OCTOBER 31ST 1517 I POSTED "95 THESES" ON INDULGENCES.

(ANSWER BELOW)

"THE ROAD TO HELL IS PAVED WITH GOOD INTENTIONS," IS NOT A QUOTE FROM THE BIBLE. IT IS FROM "Das Kapital" by KARL MARX!

SCIENCE QUIZ:

WHAT DO THE FOLLOWING HAVE IN COMMON? —...

AIR PUMP, FURNACE, CLOCK, FLYING FISH, PEACOCK, FLY, INDIAN and SERPENT—BEATER.

ANSWER: THEY ARE THE ENGLISH NAMES FOR 8 of THE 88 CONSTELLATIONS.

"HE THAT JUSTIFIETH THE WICKED, AND HE THAT CONDEMNETH THE JUST, EVEN THEY BOTH ARE ABOMINATION TO THE LORD." PROVERBS 17:15

BIBLE QUIZ: WHAT CHAPTER IN ISAIAH'S PROPHECY DESCRIBES THE SUFFERINGS OF CHRIST? ISAIAH 53

ANSWER TO "WHO AM I?" — MARTIN LUTHER

AWESOME TRUTH
by Eddie Eddings

"CHRISTIANITY IS LIKE ELECTRICITY. IT CANNOT ENTER A PERSON UNLESS IT CAN PASS THROUGH."

RICHARD C. RAINES

WHO AM I?

① I NEVER WENT TO COLLEGE YET I FOUNDED ONE IN LONDON.

② I AM A PASTOR WHO REFUSED ORDINATION.

③ I AM THE MOST PUBLISHED CHRISTIAN AUTHOR LIVING OR DEAD. (ANSWER BELOW)

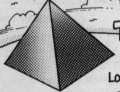

THE WORLD'S LARGEST PYRAMID IS LOCATED IN MEXICO!

THE 21ST CENTURY WILL BEGIN ON JANUARY 1ST 2001.

BIBLE QUIZ

HOW MANY BOOKS OF THE BIBLE DID JOHN WRITE?

- - - - - - - - - - - - - - - -

ANSWER: FOUR

"SHORT SINS OFTEN COST US LONG AND SAD SORROWS."

—PHILIP HENRY

THOMAS WATSON SAID...
"PRAISING GOD IS ONE OF THE HIGHEST AND PUREST ACTS OF RELIGION. IN PRAYER WE ACT LIKE MEN; IN PRAISE WE ACT LIKE ANGELS."

BENJAMIN FRANKLIN INVENTED THE HARMONICA.

ANSWER TO "WHO AM I?" — C.H. SPURGEON

20

AWESOME TRUTH by Eddie Eddings

"WE SHOULD BE ALWAYS WEARING THE GARMENT OF PRAISE, NOT JUST WAVING A PALM-BRANCH NOW AND THEN." ANDREW BONAR

WHO AM I?

① I LIKED RIDDLES.

② MY SENSUOUS LIFE BROUGHT ONE ANXIETY AFTER ANOTHER. I SHOULD HAVE LISTENED TO MY PARENTS ADVICE.

③ ONE DAY I MET A BEAUTIFUL WOMAN NAMED DELILAH. (ANSWER BELOW)

FILL in the BLANK

ACCORDING TO JOSHUA 10:11 THE AMORITES DIED IN A _____.

HAILSTORM

THE WAGES OF SIN HAVE NEVER BEEN REDUCED!

THE 1ST U.S. CHIEF JUSTICE, JOHN JAY, BOUGHT SLAVES IN ORDER TO FREE THEM.

BOTH JOHN CALVIN and JOHN KNOX ARE BURIED IN UNMARKED GRAVES!

THE "ISLANDS OF LANGERHANS" ARE A GROUP OF CELLS IN YOUR PANCREAS.

SAMSON ——— "WHO AM I?" ANSWER TO

21

AWESOME TRUTH
by Eddie Eddings

"BY NATURE WE ARE NOT ONLY **EXILES**, BUT **FUGITIVES**."
THOMAS MANTON

WHO AM I?

① MY FAITH WAS TESTED BY THE DRYING UP OF A BROOK.

② I HAD A "FIREY" PERSONALITY.

③ TWO COMPANIES OF SOLDIERS WERE DESTROYED WHEN THEY TRIED TO ARREST ME.

(ANSWER BELOW)

BIBLE QUIZ

WHO WAS THE FIRST MAN MENTIONED IN THE BIBLE TO PREACH FROM A PULPIT?

- - - - - - -

EZRA (NEHEMIAH 8:4)

ASK YOURSELF:

"WHAT KIND OF A CHURCH WOULD OURS BE IF EVERYONE WAS LIKE I AM?"

"I WILL PERMIT NO MAN TO NARROW AND DEGRADE MY SOUL BY MAKING ME HATE HIM."
—BOOKER T. WASHINGTON

SIN ALWAYS RUINS WHERE IT REIGNS!

THE **LARGEST ICEBERG** EVER RECORDED WAS AN ANTARCTIC ICEBERG SEEN IN 1956. IT COVERED 12,000 SQUARE MILES, AN AREA BIGGER THAN BELGIUM.

ANSWER TO "WHO AM I?" — ELIJAH

22

AWESOME TRUTH by Eddie Eddings

"WE ARE SO SUB-NORMAL THAT IF WE EVER BECAME NORMAL, PEOPLE WOULD THINK WE WERE ABNORMAL." *Vance Havner*

WHO AM I ?

① MY CLEAR VOICE, MASTERY OF ANGLO-SAXON, AND KEEN SENSE OF HUMOR, ALLIED TO A SURE GRASP OF SCRIPTURE AND A DEEP LOVE FOR CHRIST, PRODUCED SOME OF THE NOBLEST PREACHING OF ANY AGE.

② I SUFFERED FROM GOUT AND WOULD SOMETIMES LEAN ON A RAILING WHEN I PREACHED.

③ I AM A FIVE-POINT CALVINIST AND THE MOST QUOTED BAPTIST OF ALL TIME.   (ANSWER BELOW)

"ELECTION, SO FAR FROM UNDERMINING EVANGELISM, UNDERGIRDS IT, FOR IT PROVIDES THE ONLY HOPE OF ITS SUCCEEDING IN ITS AIM."
J. I. PACKER

BIBLE QUIZ: WHAT MAN OWNED A VINEYARD WHICH WAS COVETED BY HIS KING?

NABOTH (I KINGS 21:2)

"WOMAN WAS TAKEN OUT OF MAN; NOT OUT OF HIS HEAD TO TOP HIM, NOR OUT OF HIS FEET TO BE TRAMPLED UNDERFOOT; BUT OUT OF HIS SIDE TO BE EQUAL TO HIM, UNDER HIS ARM TO BE PROTECTED, AND NEAR HIS HEART TO BE LOVED." —— MATTHEW HENRY

"CHARM IS DECEPTIVE, AND BEAUTY IS FLEETING; BUT A WOMAN WHO FEARS THE LORD IS TO BE PRAISED." PROVERBS 31:30 (NIV)

ANSWER TO "WHO AM I ?" —— "CHARLES HADDON SPURGEON"

23

AWESOME TRUTH by Eddie Eddings

"THE WORST THING IN EVERY SIN IS THAT IT IS AGAINST GOD."
William S. Plumer

WHO AM I?

① I AM A RUGGED PROPHET WHO SUDDENLY APPEARED ON THE SCENE IN FIRST KINGS.

② TWICE, AN ANGEL BAKED ME A CAKE OF BREAD.

③ "SWING LOW SWEET CHARIOT." (ANSWER BELOW)

TRUE OR FALSE

SOLOMON'S WIFE WAS GIVEN TWO ENTIRE CITIES AS A WEDDING GIFT.

FALSE... ONLY ONE ENTIRE CITY (1 KINGS 9:16)

EVERY TRUE CHRISTIAN CAN BOAST OF HAVING THREE DEGREES:

B.A. BORN AGAIN

M.A. MIGHTILY ALTERED

D.D. DIVINELY DESTINED

REMEMBER THE WEEKDAY, TO KEEP IT HOLY.

GEORGE WASHINGTON WAS THE FIRST AMERICAN MILLIONAIRE!

ANSWER TO "WHO AM I?" — ELIJAH

AWESOME TRUTH
by Eddie Eddings

"IF THE DOCTRINE OF DIVINE SOVEREIGNTY ALONE GIVES GOD HIS RIGHTFUL PLACE, THEN IT IS ALSO TRUE THAT IT ALONE CAN SUPPLY A FIRM BASE FOR PRACTICAL RELIGION TO BUILD UPON."

A.W. PINK

WHO AM I?

① I WAS BORN THE 25th CHILD IN MY FAMILY AND BORE MY HUSBAND, SAMUEL, 19 CHILDREN.

② I AM ONE OF THE MOST NOTABLE MOTHERS IN CHRISTENDOM. I HAD TWO VERY FAMOUS SONS.

③ IT IS DIFFICULT TO IMAGINE HOW DIFFERENT THE LIVES OF JOHN AND CHARLES MIGHT HAVE BEEN LIVED WITHOUT MY DISCIPLINED UPBRINGING. (ANSWER BELOW)

THE AVERAGE MARRIED WOMAN IN 17TH CENTURY AMERICA GAVE BIRTH TO 13 CHILDREN.

SPURGEON SAID,

"WHITEFIELD AND WESLEY MIGHT PREACH THE GOSPEL BETTER THAN I DO, BUT THEY COULD NOT PREACH A BETTER GOSPEL."

TRUE OR FALSE:

THE BOOK OF ISAIAH HAS AS MANY CHAPTERS AS THERE ARE BOOKS IN THE BIBLE.

ANSWER : TRUE

THE ONLY MAMMAL THAT CAN FLY IS THE BAT.

"WITHOUT THE ABSOLUTE, WE DROWN IN THE RELATIVE. WITHOUT THE AUTHOR OF ORDER, WE SUFFOCATE IN CHAOS." R.C. SPROUL

ANSWER TO "WHO AM I?" ——— SUSANNAH WESLEY

25

AWESOME TRUTH
by Eddie Eddings

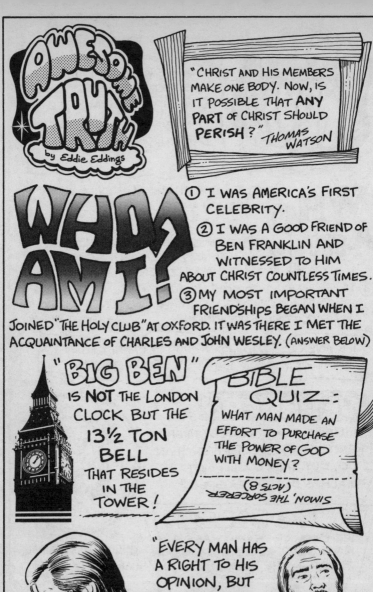

"CHRIST AND HIS MEMBERS MAKE ONE BODY. NOW, IS IT POSSIBLE THAT **ANY PART** OF CHRIST SHOULD **PERISH**?" *THOMAS WATSON*

WHO AM I?

① I WAS AMERICA'S FIRST CELEBRITY.

② I WAS A GOOD FRIEND OF BEN FRANKLIN AND WITNESSED TO HIM ABOUT CHRIST COUNTLESS TIMES.

③ MY MOST IMPORTANT FRIENDSHIPS BEGAN WHEN I JOINED "THE HOLY CLUB" AT OXFORD. IT WAS THERE I MET THE ACQUAINTANCE OF CHARLES AND JOHN WESLEY. (ANSWER BELOW)

"BIG BEN" IS **NOT** THE LONDON CLOCK BUT THE **13½ TON BELL** THAT RESIDES IN THE TOWER!

BIBLE QUIZ:

WHAT MAN MADE AN EFFORT TO PURCHASE THE POWER OF GOD WITH MONEY?

SIMON, THE SORCERER (ACTS 8)

"EVERY MAN HAS A RIGHT TO HIS OPINION, BUT NO MAN HAS A RIGHT TO BE WRONG IN HIS FACTS." BERNARD BARUCH

ANSWER TO "WHO AM I?": ——————————— GEORGE WHITEFIELD

AWESOME TRUTH by Eddie Eddings

"I CANNOT BELIEVE THAT GOD PLAYS DICE WITH THE WORLD."
ALBERT EINSTEIN

WHO AM I?

① I AM A THEOLOGIAN AND A SCIENTIST. EVERY DISCOVERY I MADE WAS BECAUSE GOD OPENED MY EYES AND UNDERSTANDING.

② I HELPED IN THE DISTRIBUTION OF BIBLES TO THE POOR AND WAS KNIGHTED BY QUEEN ANNE IN 1705.

③ I AM BEST REMEMBERED FOR THE LAW OF GRAVITY, THE INFINITESIMAL CALCULUS and THE SEPARATION OF WHITE LIGHT INTO COLORS BY THE PRISM. (ANSWER BELOW)

BIBLE QUIZ:

WHO USURPED AUTHORITY IN THE CHURCH?

DIOTREPHES (2 JOHN 9, 10)

THE ONLY TEN-LETTER WORD YOU CAN CREATE USING THE TOP LINE OF LETTERS ON A TYPEWRITER KEYBOARD IS TYPEWRITER.

THE TYPEWRITER WAS INVENTED BEFORE THE FOUNTAIN PEN.

"THERE IS DUST ENOUGH ON SOME OF YOUR BIBLES TO WRITE 'DAMNATION' WITH YOUR FINGERS."
C. H. Spurgeon

ANSWER TO "WHO AM I?" ——— SIR ISAAC NEWTON

27

AWESOME TRUTH
by Eddie Eddings

AN ANT HAS 5 NOSES

WHO AM I?

① AS A TEENAGER I WOULD NOT COMPROMISE MY RELIGIOUS CONVICTIONS.

② I, ALONE, COULD INTERPRET A KING'S DISTRESSING DREAM.

③ I CARRIED ON A CALM CONVERSATION FROM A PIT FILLED WITH FEROCIOUS BEASTS.   (ANSWER BELOW)

WOULD YOU BELIEVE... THAT A FIFTEEN LETTER WORD, WITH NO LETTERS THE SAME, IS UNCOPYRIGHTABLE?

Bible Quiz:
NAME THE ONLY WOMAN OF THE SCRIPTURES WHOSE EXACT AGE IS GIVEN.

SARAH — 127 YEARS (GENESIS 23:1)

"GOD IS BEYOND HUMAN EXAMINATION AND CAN BE KNOWN ONLY BY THOSE TO WHOM HE CHOOSES TO REVEAL HIMSELF."
GEOFFREY B. WILSON

IN THE 1830's A PATENT MEDICINE WAS SOLD UNDER THE NAME "DR. MILES' COMPOUND EXTRACT OF TOMATO." IT WAS KETCHUP.

ANSWER TO "WHO AM I?" — DANIEL

28

 **AWESOME TRUTH** by Eddie Eddings

"ALAS! OUR HEART IS OUR GREATEST ENEMY."

C.H. Spurgeon

WHO AM I?

① WHEN BUT A WEE LAD I WAS KIDNAPPED BY PIRATES AND SOLD AS A SLAVE TO AN IRISH CHIEF.

② AFTER 6 YEARS OF CAPTIVITY I ESCAPED AND RETURNED TO MY HOMELAND, SCOTLAND. LATER I RETURNED TO IRELAND TO PROCLAIM THE MESSAGE OF SALVATION.

③ I WAS THE 5th CENTURY APOSTLE TO IRELAND AND ESTABLISHED 365 CHURCHES THERE. (ANSWER BELOW)

THE HUNDRED YEAR'S WAR

LASTED 116 YEARS! (FROM 1337—1453)

BIBLE QUIZ:

WHAT EVERYDAY SUBSTANCE WAS CHANGED INTO A PLAGUE OF LICE?

DUST —(EXODUS 8:16-17)

"THE GREAT COMMISSION

IS NOT A MARKETING MANIFESTO. EVANGELISM DOES NOT REQUIRE SALESMEN, BUT PROPHETS."

JOHN MacARTHUR, Jr.

THE CHRISTIAN'S MOTTO SHOULD NOT BE "LET GO AND LET GOD" BUT "TRUST GOD AND GET GOING!"

ANSWER TO "WHO AM I?"— —PATRICK

AWESOME TRUTH
by Eddie Eddings

"IF THERE IS A SINGLE EVENT IN ALL OF THE UNIVERSE THAT CAN OCCUR OUTSIDE OF GOD'S SOVEREIGN CONTROL THEN WE CANNOT TRUST HIM." — JERRY BRIDGES

WHO AM I?

① I WAS A CONGREGATIONAL MINISTER BUT BEST KNOWN FOR MY BEST-SELLER WHICH CHALLENGED CHRISTIANS TO BASE THEIR BEHAVIOR ON THE ANSWER TO THE QUESTION, "WHAT WOULD JESUS DO?"

② MY BEST-SELLER FIRST APPEARED IN 1896 AND WAS NEVER COPYWRITED.

③ IT WAS ENTITLED, "IN HIS STEPS." (ANSWER BELOW)

NOT AS EASY AS YOU THINK QUIZ:

WHO IS BURIED IN GRANT'S TOMB?

ANSWER: NO ONE! GRANT AND HIS WIFE ARE ENTOMBED THERE.

TRUE OR FALSE

2 KINGS 19 and ISAIAH 37 ARE ALIKE.

TRUE

THE KANGAROO RAT NEVER DRINKS WATER!

THE GIDEONS INTERNATIONAL WAS ORIGINALLY CALLED "CHRISTIAN COMMERICAL MEN'S ASSOCIATION OF AMERICA." THEY PLACED THEIR FIRST BIBLE IN THE SUPERIOR HOTEL OF IRON MOUNTAIN, MONTANA IN NOVEMBER 1908. THEY NOW DISTRIBUTE BIBLES THROUGHOUT THE WORLD.

HOLY BIBLE

ANSWER TO "WHO AM I?" —— CHARLES M. SHELDON

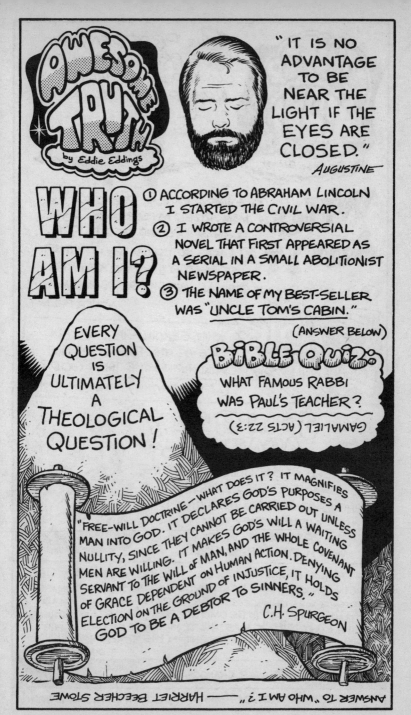

AWESOME TRUTH
by Eddie Eddings

"IT IS NO ADVANTAGE TO BE NEAR THE LIGHT IF THE EYES ARE CLOSED."
AUGUSTINE

WHO AM I?

① ACCORDING TO ABRAHAM LINCOLN I STARTED THE CIVIL WAR.

② I WROTE A CONTROVERSIAL NOVEL THAT FIRST APPEARED AS A SERIAL IN A SMALL ABOLITIONIST NEWSPAPER.

③ THE NAME OF MY BEST-SELLER WAS "UNCLE TOM'S CABIN."

(ANSWER BELOW)

EVERY QUESTION IS ULTIMATELY A THEOLOGICAL QUESTION!

BIBLE QUIZ:
WHAT FAMOUS RABBI WAS PAUL'S TEACHER?

GAMALIEL (ACTS 22:3)

"FREE-WILL DOCTRINE—WHAT DOES IT? IT MAGNIFIES MAN INTO GOD. IT DECLARES GOD'S PURPOSES A NULLITY, SINCE THEY CANNOT BE CARRIED OUT UNLESS MEN ARE WILLING. IT MAKES GOD'S WILL A WAITING SERVANT TO THE WILL OF MAN, AND THE WHOLE COVENANT OF GRACE DEPENDENT ON HUMAN ACTION. DENYING ELECTION ON THE GROUND OF INJUSTICE, IT HOLDS GOD TO BE A DEBTOR TO SINNERS."
C.H. SPURGEON

ANSWER TO "WHO AM I?" —— HARRIET BEECHER STOWE

31

by Eddie Eddings

THE PRESIDENT AND VICE-PRESIDENT OF THE UNITED STATES ARE NOT ALLOWED TO TRAVEL TOGETHER.

WHO Am I?

① I WAS A TOPICAL PREACHER WHO MEMORIZED MY SERMONS. I WAS BORN IN 1896 AND DIED IN 1978.

② I WAS NOTED FOR MY OUTSTANDING USE OF ADJECTIVES AND ADVERBS.

③ MY MOST FAMOUS SERMON WAS "PAY DAY SOMEDAY."

(ANSWER BELOW)

Bible Quiz

WHAT SEXUAL SIN DID PAUL SEE AS THE RESULT OF NOT WORSHIPING THE TRUE GOD?

(ROMANS 1:26-27) HOMOSEXUALITY

IT WAS **JOHN QUINCY ADAMS**, THE 6th ☆ PRESIDENT OF THE UNITED STATES, WHO SUPERVISED THE ESTABLISHMENT OF THE SMITHSONIAN INSTITUTION.

☆ HE WAS THE ONLY PRESIDENT WHO WAS A PUBLISHED POET.

"IF PRAYER COULD HAVE BEEN DISPENSED WITH IN ANY LIFE, SURELY IT WOULD HAVE BEEN IN THAT OF THE SINLESS SON OF MAN. IF PRAYER WAS UNNECESSARY OR UNREASONABLE, WE WOULD NATURALLY EXPECT IT TO BE OMITTED FROM HIS LIFE AND TEACHING. ON THE CONTRARY, IT WAS THE DOMINANT FEATURE OF HIS LIFE AND A RECURRENT ELEMENT IN HIS TEACHING."

J. OSWALD SANDERS

PRAYER CHANGES _YOU_!

ANSWER TO "WHO AM I?" ——— ROBERT G. LEE

32

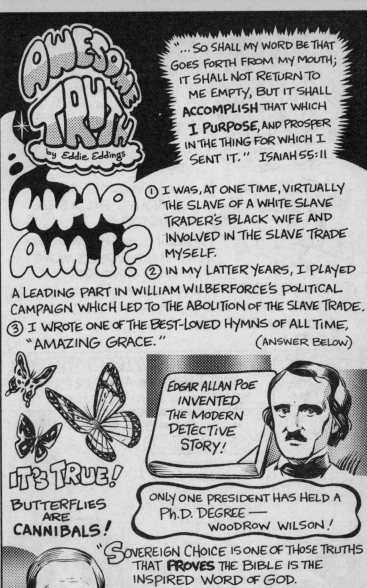

AWESOME TRUTH
by Eddie Eddings

"...SO SHALL MY WORD BE THAT GOES FORTH FROM MY MOUTH; IT SHALL NOT RETURN TO ME EMPTY, BUT IT SHALL **ACCOMPLISH** THAT WHICH **I PURPOSE**, AND PROSPER IN THE THING FOR WHICH I SENT IT." ISAIAH 55:11

WHO AM I?

① I WAS, AT ONE TIME, VIRTUALLY THE SLAVE OF A WHITE SLAVE TRADER'S BLACK WIFE AND INVOLVED IN THE SLAVE TRADE MYSELF.

② IN MY LATTER YEARS, I PLAYED A LEADING PART IN WILLIAM WILBERFORCE'S POLITICAL CAMPAIGN WHICH LED TO THE ABOLITION OF THE SLAVE TRADE.

③ I WROTE ONE OF THE BEST-LOVED HYMNS OF ALL TIME, "AMAZING GRACE." (ANSWER BELOW)

EDGAR ALLAN POE INVENTED THE MODERN DETECTIVE STORY!

IT'S TRUE!
BUTTERFLIES ARE CANNIBALS!

ONLY ONE PRESIDENT HAS HELD A Ph.D. DEGREE — WOODROW WILSON!

"SOVEREIGN CHOICE IS ONE OF THOSE TRUTHS THAT **PROVES** THE BIBLE IS THE INSPIRED WORD OF GOD. IT IS NOT A TRUTH HUMAN REASON **WOULD** OR **COULD** INVENT. THE **ONLY** REASON ANYONE BELIEVES IT IS THAT IT IS **SO CLEARLY REVEALED** IN THE WORD OF GOD." — JOHN MacARTHUR, Jr.

ANSWER TO "WHO AM I ?" —— JOHN NEWTON

AWESOME TRUTH
by Eddie Eddings

"OF ALL THE DOCTRINES OF THE BIBLE NONE IS SO OFFENSIVE TO HUMAN NATURE AS THE DOCTRINE OF GOD'S SOVEREIGNTY."
J.C. RYLE

WHO AM I?

① I AM AMONG THE MOST CELEBRATED FIRED MEN IN HISTORY

② EVEN THOUGH I WORKED WITH COWBOYS I WORE A DIFFERENT HAT.

③ AFTER I GAVE MY LIFE TO CHRIST THERE WAS AN ALMOST INSTANTANEOUS CHANGE IN MY PRIORITIES. GOD CAME FIRST, THEN MY FAMILY, AND **THEN** FOOTBALL.

(ANSWER BELOW)

BIBLE QUIZ

THE AUTHOR OF "ROBINSON CRUSOE," DANIEL DEFOE, WAS A MASTER ESPIONAGE AGENT FOR AT LEAST A DECADE!

HOW OLD WAS ABRAHAM WHEN ISAAC WAS BORN?

(GENESIS 21:5)
001

GENERAL JAMES GARFIELD (LATER PRESIDENT OF THE UNITED STATES) VISITED LONDON TO HEAR SPURGEON PREACH!

OHIO HAS THE ONLY NON-RECTANGULAR STATE FLAG!

C.H. SPURGEON

GOD ORDAINS NOT ONLY ENDS, BUT ALSO THE MEANS TO THOSE ENDS.

ANSWER TO "WHO AM I?" — TOM LANDRY

34

AWESOME TRUTH by Eddie Eddings

"BE STILL AND KNOW THAT I AM GOD. I WILL BE EXALTED AMONG THE NATIONS, I WILL BE EXALTED IN THE EARTH."

PSALM 46:10

WHO AM I?

① I HAD A "WHIRLWIND" KIND OF LIFE AND DEPARTURE.

② I THREW MY CLOAK ON A FARMER WHOSE NAME WAS A LOT LIKE MY OWN.

③ I CHALLENGED 850 FALSE PROPHETS TO A DUEL.

(ANSWER BELOW)

THE "D" IN D-DAY STANDS FOR "DAY".

THE FIRST AUTOMOBILES WERE DESIGNED TO LOOK LIKE HORSE BUGGIES. THEY WERE, IN FACT, CALLED HORSELESS CARRIAGES AND THE FIRST GARAGES, AUTOMOBILE STABLES!

BIBLE QUIZ: WHERE WERE THE DISCIPLES FIRST CALLED CHRISTIANS?

(ACTS 11:26) Antioch

"COLUMBUS, WHEN HE DISCOVERED AMERICA, COULD NOT HAVE BEEN SO OVERJOYED AS MY HEART WAS WHEN I LEARNED THE LESSON OF THOSE WORDS, 'YEA, I HAVE LOVED THEE WITH AN EVERLASTING LOVE: THEREFORE WITH LOVINGKINDNESS HAVE I DRAWN THEE.'"

C.H. SPURGEON

ANSWER TO "WHO AM I?" — ELIJAH

35

AWESOME TRUTH by Eddie Eddings

"IF SPORTING EVENTS ARE AS IMPORTANT TO YOU AS SPIRITUAL PROGRESS, YOU ARE BACKSLIDDEN."

RICHARD OWEN ROBERTS

WHO AM I?

1. I LIVED IN THE WORST CITY IN THE BOOK OF GENESIS.
2. THERE'S A DEFINITE LESSON IN MY LIFE ABOUT RUNNING FROM WRONG...EVEN IF OTHERS DON'T!
3. JESUS MENTIONED MY WIFE IN LUKE 17:32 AS A WARNING! ———————— (ANSWER BELOW)

IT'S A FACT!

TO CURE HICCUPS EAT A BANANA!

SOMETHING TO THINK ABOUT!

"WHO CAN SPEAK AND HAVE IT HAPPEN IF THE LORD HAS NOT DECREED IT?"

LAMENTATIONS 3:37

GEORGE WASHINGTON HAS NO MIDDLE NAME OR INITIAL!

"NOTHING IS SO IMPORTANT TO ANY INDIVIDUAL AS TO ESCAPE THE WRATH OF GOD, WHETHER THE PERSON IS AWARE OF THAT NEED OR NOT. ALTHOUGH PERSONS OUTSIDE OF CHRIST MAY BE UNAWARE OF THEIR DANGER, THERE IS NO EXCUSE FOR CHRISTIANS TO BE UNAWARE OF IT. IT SHOULD IMPEL ALL OF US WHO HAVE FOUND THE GRACE OF GOD IN CHRIST TO SPEAK THE GOSPEL AS WISELY, WIDELY AND RELEVANTLY AS WE CAN."

James Montgomery Boice

ANSWER TO "WHO AM I?" — LOT

36

by Eddie Eddings

"THE BOOK TO READ IS NOT ONE WHICH THINKS FOR YOU, BUT THE ONE WHICH MAKES YOU THINK. NO BOOK IN THE WORLD EQUALS THE BIBLE FOR THAT."

James McCosh

1 I WAS DIVINELY CHOSEN TO BE A KING BUT FOR A WHILE BECAME A **FUGITIVE.**

2 I SHOWED GREAT COURAGE AS A SHEPHERD BOY.

3 I AM THE MOST FAMOUS ANCESTOR OF JESUS CHRIST.

(ANSWER BELOW)

THE TEN COMMANDMENTS
IN RHYME

1. THOU NO GODS SHALT HAVE BUT ME.
2. BEFORE NO IDOL BOW THE KNEE.
3. TAKE NOT THE NAME OF GOD IN VAIN.
4. DARE NOT THE SABBATH DAY PROFANE.
5. GIVE TO THY PARENTS HONOR DUE.
6. TAKE HEED THAT THOU NO MURDER DO.
7. ABSTAIN FROM WORDS AND DEEDS UNCLEAN.
8. STEAL NOT, FOR THOU BY GOD ART SEEN.
9. TELL NO WILLFUL LIE AND LOVE IT.
10. WHAT IS THY NEIGHBORS DO NOT COVET.

BIBLE QUIZ

HOW OLD WAS METHUSELAH WHEN HE DIED ?

(GENESIS 5:27) 969

PRESIDENT ULYSSES S. GRANT HAD HIS MEMOIRS PUBLISHED BY MARK TWAIN !

ANSWER TO "WHO AM I ?" —— DAVID

AWESOME TRUTH
by Eddie Eddings

"MY HOPE IN THE ONE WHO CREATED US ALL SUSTAINS ME: HE IS AN EVER PRESENT HELP IN TROUBLE.... WHEN I WAS EXTREMELY DEPRESSED, HE RAISED ME WITH HIS RIGHT HAND, SAYING, 'O MAN OF LITTLE FAITH, GET UP, IT IS I; DO NOT BE AFRAID.'"

CHRISTOPHER COLUMBUS

WHO AM I?

① MY FAME SPREAD THROUGHOUT THE WORLD IN 1 KINGS 4:29-34.
② I CARRIED OUT THE PLANS OF MY FATHER CONCERNING THE TEMPLE.
③ I WROTE A LOVE "SONG" THAT HAS "S.O.S." AS IT'S INITIALS.   (ANSWER BELOW)

BIBLE QUIZ: WHAT STRANGE PHENOMENON ACCOMPANIED THE PLAGUE OF HAIL IN EGYPT?

ANSWER: (EXODUS 9:23) FIRE THAT RAN ALONG THE GROUND

BELIEVE IT OR NOT...

EXCEPT FOR THE LORD'S MERCIES, EVERY HUMAN BEING IN THE WORLD WOULD BE CONSUMED!
— SEE LAMENTATIONS 3:22 —

ONE-FOURTH OF ALL THE BONES IN THE HUMAN BODY ARE LOCATED IN THE FEET.

WHAT ARE **YOU** DOING TO ENCOURAGE OTHERS?

JOHN QUINCY ADAMS NAMED ONE OF HIS SONS GEORGE WASHINGTON

ANSWER TO "WHO AM I?" — SOLOMON

38

AWESOME TRUTH by Eddie Eddings

"GOD IS STILL ON THE THRONE, WE'RE STILL ON HIS FOOTSTOOL, AND THERE'S ONLY A KNEE'S DISTANCE BETWEEN." — JIM ELLIOT

WHO AM I?

① ON MY JOURNEY TO AMERICA I MET A COMPANY OF MORAVIANS WHOSE SIMPLE FAITH MADE A CONSIDERABLE IMPRESSION ON ME.

② I KEPT A DAILY JOURNAL OF MY EVANGELISTIC JOURNEYS COVERING MORE THAN 50 YEARS.

③ I AM CONSIDERED BY MANY TO BE THE LEADER AND FOUNDER OF METHODISM, THOUGH AMONG MY CONTEMPORARIES IT WAS WHITEFIELD WHO WAS SO REGARDED.

(ANSWER BELOW)

BIBLE QUIZ

HOW MANY SOLDIERS WERE ENGAGED IN THE DARK DEED OF CRUCIFYING JESUS?

———————

FOUR (JOHN 19:23)

THE **SANDWICH** WAS NAMED AFTER A NOTORIOUS 18th CENTURY GAMBLER, JOHN MONTAGU, FOURTH EARL OF SANDWICH!

"WHAT WE CALL REVIVAL IS SIMPLY A RETURN TO NORMAL NEW TESTAMENT CHRISTIANITY." — HAVNER

97% OF ALL PEOPLE OFFERED A NEW PEN TO TRY, WRITE THEIR OWN NAME.

ANSWER TO "WHO AM I?" ——— JOHN WESLEY

AWESOME TRUTH

by Eddie Eddings

"LET THEM FEAR **DEATH** WHO DO NOT FEAR SIN."
THOMAS WATSON

WHO AM I?

① I REFUSED THE TITLE OF "REVEREND" AS A MATTER OF PRINCIPLE, WROTE MANY HYMNS, AND WAS RESPONSIBLE FOR FOUNDING AN ORPHANAGE IN 1867.

② THE TABERNACLE WHEREIN I PREACHED IS STILL LOCATED AT ELEPHANT AND CASTLE IN LONDON.

③ I DIED AT MENTONE IN FRANCE AFTER A LENGTHY ILLNESS.

(ANSWER BELOW)

BIBLE QUIZ

WHAT PROPHET WAS MARRIED TO A PROPHETESS?

(ISAIAH 8:3) ISAIAH

AMERICA'S GOLD IS KEPT AT FT. KNOX. IT'S SILVER IS KEPT AT WEST POINT.

YOU HAVE TO COUNT ALL THE WAY TO ONE THOUSAND BEFORE THE LETTER "A" IS USED IN SPELLING A NUMBER.

"LET IT NOT BE FORGOTTEN ... GOD'S PROVIDENCES ARE BUT THE MANIFESTATIONS OF HIS DECREES: WHAT GOD DOES IN TIME IS ONLY WHAT HE PURPOSED IN ETERNITY — HIS OWN WILL BEING THE ALONE CAUSE OF ALL HIS ACTS AND WORKS."
A.W. PINK

ANSWER TO "WHO AM I?" — C.H. SPURGEON

40

AWESOME TRUTH
by Eddie Eddings

"THE TREATMENT OF OUR LORD JESUS CHRIST BY MEN IS THE CLEAREST PROOF OF TOTAL DEPRAVITY.

THOSE MUST BE STONY HEARTS INDEED WHICH CAN LAUGH AT A DYING SAVIOR AND MOCK EVEN HIS FAITH IN GOD!"

C.H. SPURGEON

WHO am i?

① I HAD THE BEST EDUCATION MONEY COULD BUY BUT I HAD TROUBLE SPEAKING.

② I NOTICED A DESERT SHRUB BURNING WITHOUT BEING DESTROYED.

③ IN A FIT OF RAGE I STRUCK A ROCK TWICE. (ANSWER BELOW)

THE WAY A SHADOW MOVES AROUND A **SUNDIAL** (CLOCKWISE) INFLUENCED THE DIRECTION HANDS MOVE AROUND A **CLOCK**.

BIBLE QUIZ: WHAT DOES SATAN MASQUERADE AS IN THE PRESENT WORLD?

(AN ANGEL OF LIGHT) (2 CORINTHIANS 11:14)

TRUE! ANTS DO NOT SLEEP!

QUESTION: THEN WHY ARE THERE ANT "BEDS"?

WHAT ON EARTH ARE YOU DOING FOR HEAVEN'S SAKE?

90% OF ALL SPECIES THAT HAVE BECOME EXTINCT HAVE BEEN BIRDS!

MOSES ——— ANSWER TO "WHO AM I?"

41

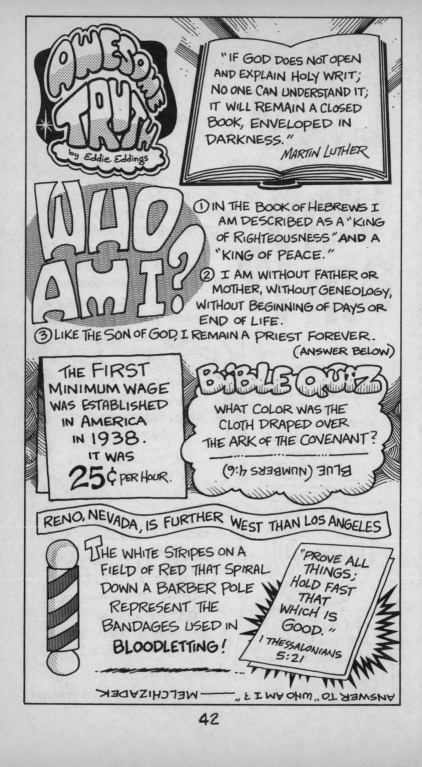

AWESOME TRUTH
by Eddie Eddings

"IF GOD DOES NOT OPEN AND EXPLAIN HOLY WRIT; NO ONE CAN UNDERSTAND IT; IT WILL REMAIN A CLOSED BOOK, ENVELOPED IN DARKNESS."
MARTIN LUTHER

WHO AM I?

① IN THE BOOK OF HEBREWS I AM DESCRIBED AS A "KING OF RIGHTEOUSNESS" AND A "KING OF PEACE."

② I AM WITHOUT FATHER OR MOTHER, WITHOUT GENEOLOGY, WITHOUT BEGINNING OF DAYS OR END OF LIFE.

③ LIKE THE SON OF GOD, I REMAIN A PRIEST FOREVER.

(ANSWER BELOW)

THE FIRST MINIMUM WAGE WAS ESTABLISHED IN AMERICA IN 1938. IT WAS 25¢ PER HOUR.

BIBLE QUIZ

WHAT COLOR WAS THE CLOTH DRAPED OVER THE ARK OF THE COVENANT?

———

BLUE (NUMBERS 4:6)

RENO, NEVADA, IS FURTHER WEST THAN LOS ANGELES

THE WHITE STRIPES ON A FIELD OF RED THAT SPIRAL DOWN A BARBER POLE REPRESENT THE BANDAGES USED IN BLOODLETTING!

"PROVE ALL THINGS; HOLD FAST THAT WHICH IS GOOD."
1 THESSALONIANS 5:21

ANSWER TO "WHO AM I?" ——— MELCHIZADEK

42

AWESOME TRUTH by Eddie Eddings

William Jenkyn said the cure for pride was to remember "our Father was ADAM, our GRANDFATHER DUST, our GREAT-GRANDFATHER NOTHING."

WHO AM I?

① I TRANSLATED THE BIBLE INTO THE DIALECT OF THE ALGONQUIN INDIANS.

② I ABANDONED A LIFE OF SCHOLARSHIP TO BE A MISSIONARY TO THE INDIANS.

③ I WAS KNOWN AS "THE APOSTLE TO THE INDIANS" AND ESTABLISHED THE FIRST INDIAN CHURCH IN 1660.   (ANSWER BELOW)

BIBLE QUIZ: IS THERE A WOMAN IN THE BIBLE NAMED NOAH?

YES (NUMBERS 26:33)

THE **HORNS** OF THE RHINOCEROS ARE ACTUALLY MADE UP OF COMPACTED HAIR!

WILLIAM GRIMSHAW

(1708-1763) A CIRCUIT RIDER BEFORE WESLEY, WAS BURIED ACCORDING TO HIS SPECIFICATIONS: "IN A CHEAP, VERY PLAIN COFFIN, PAINTED AND THEN CLEARLY LETTERED WITH MY FAVORITE TEXT — PHILIPPIANS 1:21."

"TO ME TO LIVE IS CHRIST, AND TO DIE IS GAIN." PHILIPPIANS 1:21

ANSWER TO "WHO AM I?" ————— JOHN ELIOT

AWESOME TRUTH
by Eddie Eddings

"THE BIG QUESTION TODAY IS NOT, 'IS GOD SPEAKING?' BUT 'ARE YOU LISTENING?'"

VANCE HAVNER

READ GOD'S WORD

WHO AM I?

① I WAS ONE OF THE GREATEST POLITICAL REFORMERS THE ENGLISH-SPEAKING PEOPLES HAVE EVER PRODUCED.

② JOHN NEWTON URGED ME TO STAY IN POLITICS, BELIEVING THAT GOD MIGHT HAVE RAISED ME UP FOR A PURPOSE.

③ I TOOK UP THE CAUSE OF THE SLAVES IN THE BRITISH HOUSE OF COMMONS AND SAW THE ABOLITION OF SLAVERY IN MY LIFETIME.

(ANSWER BELOW)

SPAGHETTI WAS INVENTED BY THE CHINESE!

BIBLE QUIZ
WHAT WAS THE PENALTY FOR KIDNAPPING IN THE OLD TESTAMENT?

DEATH (EXODUS 21:16)

OUR ORIGINAL PARENTS, **ADAM** and **EVE** DID NOT HAVE NAVELS!

"BLESSED IS HE THAT CONSIDERETH THE POOR; THE LORD WILL DELIVER HIM IN TIME OF TROUBLE." PSALM 41:1

THE STATUE OF LIBERTY IS **NOT** THAT MONUMENT'S NAME. IT IS "LIBERTY ENLIGHTENING THE WORLD"!

ANSWER TO "WHO AM I?" ———— WILLIAM WILBERFORCE

44

AWESOME TRUTH by Eddie Eddings

> "SPIRITUAL AWAKENING DOES NOT TAKE PLACE APART FROM BIBLICAL TRUTH."
>
> KENNETH GOOD

WHO AM I?

① MY NAME IS HOSHEA, SON OF NUN, BUT MOSES RE-NAMED ME.

② I ACCOMPANIED MOSES PARTWAY UP MT. SINAI WHEN THE DECALOGUE WAS GIVEN.

③ I WAS DIVINELY APPOINTED AND ORDAINED AS SUCCESSOR OF MOSES. (ANSWER BELOW)

THE FASTEST ANIMAL

IS THE PEREGRINE FALCON, WHICH CAN DIVE AT SPEEDS UP TO **240** MILES AN HOUR!

THE ONLY PRESIDENT TO WIN A PULITZER PRIZE WAS JOHN F. KENNEDY.

BIBLE QUIZ:

WHAT BOOK OF THE BIBLE RECORDS THE SHORTEST PRAYER?

"LORD, SAVE ME!" MATTHEW (14:30)

THE FIRST LESSON IN

CALVINISTIC THEOLOGY CHARLES HADDON SPURGEON EVER RECEIVED WAS FROM AN **OLD COOK**, MARY KING.

"I DO BELIEVE THAT I LEARNED MORE FROM HER THAN I SHOULD HAVE LEARNED FROM ANY SIX DOCTORS OF DIVINITY OF THE SORT WE HAVE NOWADAYS." ——— C.H. SPURGEON

ANSWER TO "WHO AM I?" ——— JOSHUA

45

AWESOME TRUTH by Eddie Eddings

"WHAT IS OFFERED TO MEN IN THE GOSPEL? IT IS NOT THE POSSIBILITY OF SALVATION, NOT SIMPLY THE OPPORTUNITY OF SALVATION. WHAT IS OFFERED IS SALVATION."
JOHN MURRAY

WHO AM I?

① IN THE EARLY YEARS OF MY REIGN, I MADE A FOOLISH MISTAKE IN CHOOSING A PAGAN KING'S DAUGHTER FOR MY WIFE.

② IN MY LATER YEARS I WAS INFLUENCED BY MY MANY WIVES TO TURN FROM GOD.

③ I AM KNOWN AS THE WISEST MAN, YET MY WISDOM DID NOT TEACH ME SELF-CONTROL.

(ANSWER BELOW)

BIBLE QUIZ

WHAT BOOK TELLS US THAT GOD MAKES "WEIGHT FOR THE WINDS"?
(A FACT THAT WAS NOT SCIENTIFICALLY ESTABLISHED UNTIL THE 17th CENTURY BY PASCAL.)

THE Book of JOB (SEE CHAPTER 28 VERSE 25)

A DECK OF PLAYING CARDS CONTAIN 52 CARDS, and "ACE, TWO, THREE, FOUR, FIVE, SIX, SEVEN, EIGHT, NINE, TEN, JACK, QUEEN, KING" ADD UP TO EXACTLY 52 LETTERS.

RONALD REAGAN IS THE OLDEST MAN TO HAVE BEEN ELECTED PRESIDENT

SOLOMON — ANSWER TO "WHO AM I?"

AWESOME TRUTH by Eddie Eddings

"WHAT PHILOSOPHY IS STRIVING TO FIND, THEOLOGY ASSERTS HAS BEEN FOUND."

AUGUSTUS H. STRONG

WHO AM I?

① I WAS A KEY FIGURE IN THE INTELLECTUAL HISTORY OF AMERICAN THEOLOGY.

② I PLAYED A DOMINANT ROLE IN LEADING AND GUIDING THE GREAT AWAKENING.

③ MY MOST NOTABLE SERMON WAS ENTITLED, "SINNERS IN THE HANDS OF AN ANGRY GOD." (ANSWER BELOW)

"GOD CHOSE YOU FROM THE BEGINNING UNTO SALVATION IN SANCTIFICATION OF THE SPIRIT AND BELIEF OF THE TRUTH."

2 THESSALONIANS 2:13

BIBLE QUIZ

WHOSE HANDS WERE COVERED WITH HAIR?

ESAU (GENESIS 27:13)

"IN THE WOUNDS OF CHRIST ALONE IS PREDESTINATION FOUND AND UNDERSTOOD." —— MARTIN LUTHER

THE STATUE OF LIBERTY ORIGINALLY WAS TO BE SET UP AT THE SUEZ CANAL!

IN 1803 THOMAS JEFFERSON PURCHASED THE LOUISIANA TERRITORY FROM NAPOLEON AT 4¢ an ACRE.

ANSWER TO "WHO AM I?" —— JONATHAN EDWARDS

47

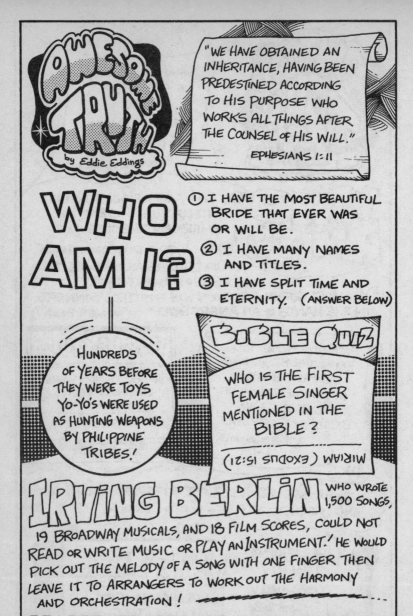

AWESOME TRUTH by Eddie Eddings

"WE HAVE OBTAINED AN INHERITANCE, HAVING BEEN PREDESTINED ACCORDING TO HIS PURPOSE WHO WORKS ALL THINGS AFTER THE COUNSEL OF HIS WILL."

EPHESIANS 1:11

WHO AM I?

1. I HAVE THE MOST BEAUTIFUL BRIDE THAT EVER WAS OR WILL BE.
2. I HAVE MANY NAMES AND TITLES.
3. I HAVE SPLIT TIME AND ETERNITY. (ANSWER BELOW)

HUNDREDS OF YEARS BEFORE THEY WERE TOYS YO-YO'S WERE USED AS HUNTING WEAPONS BY PHILIPPINE TRIBES!

BIBLE QUIZ

WHO IS THE FIRST FEMALE SINGER MENTIONED IN THE BIBLE?

MIRIAM (EXODUS 15:21)

IRVING BERLIN WHO WROTE 1,500 SONGS,

19 BROADWAY MUSICALS, AND 18 FILM SCORES, COULD NOT READ OR WRITE MUSIC OR PLAY AN INSTRUMENT! HE WOULD PICK OUT THE MELODY OF A SONG WITH ONE FINGER THEN LEAVE IT TO ARRANGERS TO WORK OUT THE HARMONY AND ORCHESTRATION!

ANSWER TO "WHO AM I?"——THE LORD JESUS CHRIST

48

AWESOME TRUTH by Eddie Eddings

IN EARLIER TIMES, THE YEAR **1666 A.D.** WAS EXPECTED TO BE THE END OF THE WORLD!

IN ROMAN NUMBERS THE YEAR REPRESENTED ALL THE DIGITS IN DESCENDING ORDER — MDCLXVI

WHO AM I?

① I WAS A SCOTTISH THEOLOGIAN AND MISSIONARY.

② A CALVINIST, ASSOCIATED WITH THE FREE CHURCH, AND A MAN OF METICULOUS MIND.

③ I AM BEST KNOWN FOR MY COMPREHENSIVE "ANALYTICAL CONCORDANCE TO THE HOLY BIBLE" PUBLISHED IN 1879.   (ANSWER BELOW)

THERE ARE 44,500 "LETTERS" (OR CHARACTERS) IN THE CHINESE "ALPHABET."

BIBLE QUIZ:

WHAT PROPHET'S WORD CAUSED THE SYRIAN SOLDIERS TO BE STRUCK BLIND?

(ELISHA'S (2 KINGS 6:18-23))

"**T**HE VERY SCIENCES FROM WHICH OBJECTIONS HAVE BEEN BROUGHT AGAINST RELIGION HAVE, BY THEIR OWN PROGRESS, REMOVED THOSE OBJECTIONS, AND IN THE END FURNISHED FULL CONFIRMATION OF THE INSPIRED WORD OF GOD." TRYON EDWARDS

"I ONLY TRACE THE LINES THAT FLOW FROM GOD." ALBERT EINSTEIN

ANSWER TO "WHO AM I?" ——— ROBERT YOUNG

49

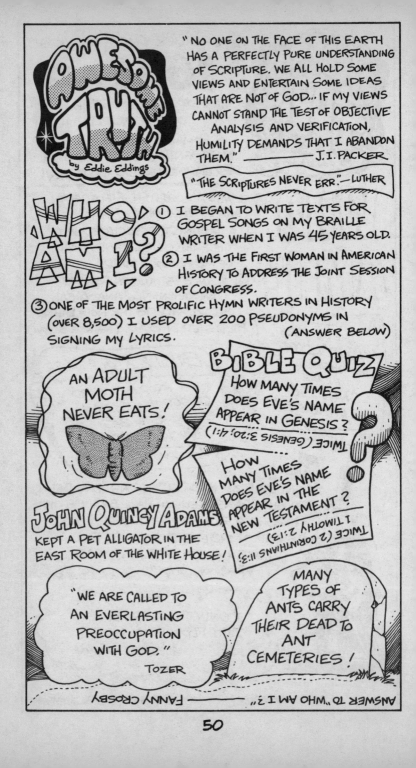

AWESOME TRUTH

by Eddie Eddings

WHO AM I?

① I WAS BORN AT RAMAH NEAR THE CLOSE OF THE PERIOD OF THE JUDGES.

② MY MOTHER PRESENTED ME TO THE PRIEST, ELI, AS SOON AS I WAS WEANED.

③ I WAS ONE OF THE GREATEST OF ALL THE PROPHETS, AND HAD THE HONOR OF ANOINTING THE FIRST TWO KINGS OF ISRAEL.

(ANSWER BELOW)

BIBLE QUIZ

FOR WHAT STRANGE OFFENSE WAS A PROPHET KILLED BY A LION?

(HE REFUSED THE REQUEST OF ANOTHER PROPHET TO HIT HIM (1 KINGS 20:35-36).)

THE RICKSHAW

WAS INVENTED BY AN AMERICAN!

JONATHAN SCOBIE, A BAPTIST MINISTER LIVING IN JAPAN, BUILT THE FIRST MODEL IN 1869 IN ORDER TO TRANSPORT HIS INVALID WIFE THROUGH THE CITY STREETS.

"I HAVE READ OF A WOMAN WHO WENT TO A PSYCHIATRIST WEARING A STRIP OF BACON OVER EACH EAR AND A FRIED EGG ON TOP OF HER HEAD. SHE SAID TO HIM... 'I'VE COME TO SEE YOU ABOUT MY BROTHER.' I HAVE HEARD PEOPLE PRAY WHO WERE CONSCIOUS OF OTHER PEOPLE'S FAULTS BUT NOT OF THEIR OWN." —VANCE HAVNER

ANSWER TO "WHO AM I?" — SAMUEL

51

by Eddie Eddings

CHRISTIANS MAY NOT SEE EYE TO EYE, BUT THEY CAN WALK ARM IN ARM.

WHO AM I?

① MANY OF MY BOOKS WERE DESIGNED TO REMOVE OBSTACLES FACING THE CHRISTIAN IN AN AGNOSTIC AGE OF SCIENTIFIC MATERIALISM. "MIRACLES" WAS ONE SUCH BOOK.

② MOST OF MY LIFE WAS SPENT IN QUIET BACHERLORHOOD, BUT IN 1956 I MARRIED JOY.

③ MY SEVEN BOOKS OF THE LAND OF NARNIA HAVE BECOME MODERN CHILDREN'S CLASSICS. (ANSWER BELOW)

BIBLE QUIZ

WHAT WAS THE FIRST CITY CALLED?

(ENOCH, NAMED AFTER CAIN'S SON (GENESIS 4:17)

"THE WORST THING WE CAN BRING TO A RELIGIOUS CONTROVERSY IS ANGER."
MATTHEW HENRY

THE ONLY CELLS IN THE HUMAN BODY THAT DON'T REGENERATE ARE THE BRAIN CELLS.

DID GOD GIVE HIS SON THAT "WHOSOEVER" MIGHT NOT PERISH, OR THAT "WHOSOEVER BELIEVETH IN HIM" MIGHT NOT PERISH?

96 OF THE WORLD'S 109 TALLEST PEAKS ARE LOCATED IN THE HIMALAYAS.

ANSWER TO "WHO AM I?" — C.S. LEWIS

AWESOME TRUTH
by Eddie Eddings

"WHEN YOU EDUCATE A MAN IN MIND AND NOT IN MORALS YOU EDUCATE A MENACE TO SOCIETY."

FRANKLIN D. ROOSEVELT

WHO AM I?

① I LOST MY EYESIGHT AT SIX WEEKS OLD IN 1823.

② IN 1858 I MARRIED A BLIND MUSICIAN AND TOGETHER WE PRODUCED A NUMBER OF HYMNS.

③ MY HYMNS ARE SOME OF THE MOST LOVED TODAY.

(ANSWER BELOW)

BIBLE QUIZ

WHO BUILT NINEVEH?

NIMROD (GENESIS 10:11)

THE FIRST AMERICAN TO HAVE PLUMBING INSTALLED IN HIS HOME WAS HENRY WADSWORTH LONGFELLOW IN 1840.

Dilemma

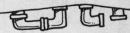

"God imposed His wrath due unto, and Christ underwent the pains of hell for, either

A. ALL the sins of ALL men, B. ALL the sins of SOME men, or C. SOME of the sins of ALL men.

• If the last is true, <u>Some of the sins of ALL men</u>, then all men have some sins to answer for, and no man shall be saved.
• If the second is true, <u>ALL the sins of SOME men</u>, which we affirm, then Christ actually suffered in the room and stead of all the elect in the world.
• If the first is true, <u>ALL the sins of ALL men</u>, why, then, are not all freed from the punishment of ALL their sins?

You will say, "Because of their unbelief, they will not believe."

<u>*BUT THIS UNBELIEF...IS IT A SIN, OR NOT?*</u>

If not...why should they be punished for it?

If it be, then Christ underwent punishment to it, or not.

If so, then why must that hinder them more than their other sins for which He died from partaking of the fruit of his death?

If He did not, then He did not die for all their sins. Let them choose which part they will." —*JOHN OWEN*

ANSWER TO "WHO AM I?": FANNY CROSBY

AWESOME TRUTH

by Eddie Eddings

"ALL TELEVISION IS EDUCATIONAL TELEVISION. THE ONLY QUESTION IS, WHAT IS IT TEACHING."

NICHOLAS JOHNSON

WHO AM I?

① MY BROTHER AND I BOTH HAD "STORMY" TEMPERS. BUT JESUS EVENTUALLY TRANSFORMED OUR TEMPESTUOUS NATURE INTO A LOVING ONE.

② I AM CALLED "THE APOSTLE OF LOVE" AND "THE BELOVED DISCIPLE."

③ I WROTE ONE OF THE GOSPELS. —— (ANSWER BELOW)

"AN IDOL OF THE MIND IS AS OFFENSIVE TO GOD AS AN IDOL OF THE HAND."

A.W. TOZER

BIBLE QUIZ: WHAT WAS THE NAME OF TIMOTHY'S GRANDMOTHER?

SIOT

THE **KIWI** IS THE ONLY BIRD THAT HAS NOSTRILS AT THE END OF ITS BILL!

THERE ARE 293 WAYS TO MAKE CHANGE FOR A DOLLAR.

"JOHN THE BAPTIST DID NOT OFFER A FREE CAMEL RIDE TO WHOEVER BROUGHT THE MOST PEOPLE TO HEAR HIM PREACH, NOR DID HE GIVE AN AUTOGRAPHED COPY OF ISAIAH TO THE OLDEST GRANDMOTHER PRESENT. HE WAS HIS OWN PUBLICITY AND NEEDED NO PRESS AGENT." —VANCE HAVNER

ANSWER TO "WHO AM I?" —— JOHN

AWESOME TRUTH by Eddie Eddings

AN OPEN MIND IS LIKE AN OPEN WINDOW; YOU HAVE TO PUT IN SCREENS TO KEEP THE BUGS OUT!

THE SCRIPTURES ARE THE CHRISTIAN'S SCREEN.

WHO AM I?

① AN ANGEL APPEARED TO ME AND TOLD ME THAT MY PRAYERS WERE ANSWERED.

② I WAS PROMISED BY THE ANGEL THAT MY WIFE WOULD GIVE BIRTH TO A VERY REMARKABLE SON.

③ THE ABILITY TO SPEAK WAS TAKEN FROM ME UNTIL AFTER THE BIRTH OF MY SON, JOHN. (ANSWER BELOW)

BIBLE QUIZ:

WHAT IS IT THAT YOU SEE EVERY TIME YOU GO TO CHURCH, WHICH IS ONLY MENTIONED ONCE IN THE BIBLE?

PULPIT (NEHEMIAH 8:4)

" THY WORD HAVE I HID IN MINE HEART, THAT I MIGHT NOT SIN AGAINST THEE."

PSALM 119:11

WHAT IS NAPOLEON'S CONNECTION WITH THE F.B.I.?

IT WAS FOUNDED IN 1908 BY NAPOLEON'S GRANDNEPHEW, ATTORNEY GENERAL CHARLES J. BONAPARTE, DURING THE ADMINISTRATION OF THEODORE ROOSEVELT.

ANSWER TO "WHO AM I?" — ZACHARIAS

55

AWESOME TRUTH

by Eddie Eddings

"IT WERE FAR EASIER TO WRITE A BOOK OF APOSTATES IN THIS AGE THAN A BOOK OF MARTYRS."

John Trapp

WHO AM I?

① THEY SAY I AM A THEOLOGIAN'S THEOLOGIAN, ONE OF THE GREATEST IN CHRISTIAN HISTORY.

② I WAS READY FOR COLLEGE AT AGE 12 AND SLEPT AN AVERAGE OF 4 HOURS EACH NIGHT.

③ FROM 1649-1651 I SERVED AS CHAPLAIN WITH OLIVER CROMWELL'S ARMY. (ANSWER BELOW)

BIBLE QUIZ

HOW MANY BOOKS OF THE BIBLE END WITH A QUESTION?

Two - JONAH and NAHUM! *(shown inverted)*

WILLIAM SHAKESPEARE HAS NO LIVING DESCENDANTS.

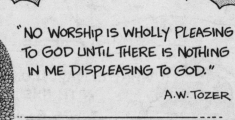

"NO WORSHIP IS WHOLLY PLEASING TO GOD UNTIL THERE IS NOTHING IN ME DISPLEASING TO GOD."

A.W. TOZER

"SHE [WISDOM] IS A TREE OF LIFE TO THOSE WHO EMBRACE HER; THOSE WHO LAY HOLD OF HER WILL BE BLESSED."

PSALM 3:18 NIV

ANSWER TO "WHO AM I?" — JOHN OWEN *(shown inverted)*

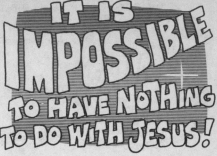

Awesome Truth by Eddie Eddings

IT IS IMPOSSIBLE TO HAVE NOTHING TO DO WITH JESUS!

WHO AM I?

1. IN 1924 I WON THE OLYMPIC GOLD MEDAL FOR THE 400-METER FINAL IN PARIS.

2. THE 1981 FILM," CHARIOTS OF FIRE," HIGHLIGHTED MY CHRISTIAN WITNESS AND CONVICTIONS.

3. IN 1943 I WAS IMPRISONED AT WEIHSIEN INTERNMENT CAMP BY THE JAPANESE BECAUSE OF MY MISSION WORK AND DIED THERE 2 YEARS LATER.

(ANSWER BELOW)

BIBLE QUIZ:

WHAT MAN PAID HIS FARE TO A CERTAIN PLACE, BUT NEVER ARRIVED?

JONAH

"JESUS CHRIST DEMANDS MORE COMPLETE ALLEGIANCE THAN ANY DICTATOR WHO EVER LIVED. THE DIFFERENCE IS, HE HAS A RIGHT TO IT."

VANCE HAVNER

"DON'T ABANDON EVANGELISM BEFORE YOU EVEN BEGIN! DON'T TRY TO CHOOSE THE ELECT! THAT HAPPENS TO BE GOD'S TASK. HOW DO YOU KNOW WHOM GOD WILL CALL TO HIMSELF? GOD HAS A SOVEREIGN PLAN CONCEIVED IN ALL WISDOM. IN THAT PLAN HE BRINGS YOU TO THE PEOPLE HE WANTS YOU TO MEET. IS IT NOT LIKELY THAT HE WILL BE GUIDING YOU TO HIS OWN SHEEP AMONG YOUR FRIENDS? BE A FRIEND WITH A DIFFERENCE. BE MORE FRIENDLY THAN YOU EVER WERE BEFORE AND PREPARE YOURSELF TO WITNESS..." —————— ———— C. JOHN MILLER

23 YEAR OLD GEORGE ARMSTRONG CUSTER WAS THE YOUNGEST MAN EVER TO BECOME A GENERAL IN THE U.S. ARMY.

ANSWER TO "WHO AM I?"——ERIC LIDDELL

AWESOME TRUTH by Eddie Eddings

"WHEN BIBLE BELIEVERS TAKE A STAND AGAINST FALSE DOCTRINE, THEY ARE ACCUSED OF 'ROCKING THE BOAT.' IT IS BETTER THAT BELIEF SHOULD ROCK THE BOAT THAN THAT UNBELIEF SHOULD WRECK THE BOAT."

Vance Havner

WHO AM I?

① MY VISION IS INSTRUMENTAL IN THE FOUNDING OF THE CHRISTIAN BOOKSELLERS ASSOCIATION.

② WANTING TO PUBLISH A CHRISTIAN MAGAZINE SIMILAR TO READER'S DIGEST I STARTED THE CHRISTIAN READER FROM MY DINING ROOM/OFFICE.

③ IN ORDER TO HELP MY OWN CHILDREN UNDERSTAND THE BIBLE, I BEGAN TO WRITE THE BEST-SELLING PARAPHRASE OF ALL TIME, THE LIVING BIBLE. *(ANSWER BELOW)*

REV. 22: 21

THE LAST WORD OF THE BIBLE IS "AMEN."

BIBLE QUIZ: WHO BURIED ISAAC?

JACOB and ESAU (GENESIS 35:29)

THE FIRST BOOK MANUSCRIPT TO BE TYPEWRITTEN WAS "THE ADVENTURES OF TOM SAWYER," BY MARK TWAIN.

BY THE WAY:

CAPTAIN ISAIAH SELLERS WAS THE FIRST TO ADOPT THE NAME MARK TWAIN. (HE WROTE A BOATING COLUMN FOR A NEW ORLEANS NEWSPAPER.) SAMUEL CLEMENS TOOK THE NAME UPON SELLERS' DEATH.

IN PROPORTION TO ITS THICKNESS, SPIDER SILK IS STRONGER THAN STEEL!

ANSWER TO "WHO AM I?" — KEN TAYLOR

58

AWESOME TRUTH
by Eddie Eddings

WHO AM I?

① I WAS BORN IN BETHLEHEM.

② I WAS A GOOD SHEPHERD.

③ MY MUSIC WOULD MAKE AN EVIL SPIRIT DEPART.
(I SAMUEL 16:23)
(ANSWER BELOW)

THAT'S A FACT! ➡ FEMALE ARMADILLOS HAVE EXACTLY FOUR BABIES AT A TIME AND THEY ARE ALWAYS THE SAME SEX!

BIBLE QUIZ

WHO SENT SPIES TO WATCH JESUS?
————————————
(LUKE 20:20)
THE CHIEF PRIESTS AND SCRIBES

"THE CHRISTIAN LIFE _IS_ A BED OF ROSES—THORNS AND ALL."

DOUG BARNETT

"MANY PEOPLE TODAY WANT TO MAKE OUR GOVERNMENT THE TARGET OF THEIR MINISTRY EFFORTS, IN AN ATTEMPT TO SAVE OUR COUNTRY. THAT IS A MISDIRECTED FOCUS. IT IS THE **CHURCH** THAT GOD WANTS TO USE TO CHANGE AMERICA. TRUE CHANGE CAN ONLY COME FROM WITHIN AND ONLY GOD WORKING THROUGH THE CHURCH CAN CHANGE HEARTS IN AMERICA. SO, THE CHURCH—NOT THE GOVERNMENT—IS GOD'S PRIMARY AGENT FOR CHANGE IN THE NATION." —— STEVEN J. LAWSON

DID YOU KNOW? THE SMALLEST TREES IN THE WORLD, THE DWARF WILLOWS, ARE ONLY TWO INCHES HIGH!

ANSWER TO "WHO AM I?" —— DAVID

59

AWESOME TRUTH
by Eddie Eddings

DAY BY DAY THE MANNA FELL OH, TO LEARN THIS LESSON WELL.

WHO AM I?

① I PERFORMED A GREATER NUMBER OF MIRACLES THAN ANY OTHER PROPHET EXCEPT MOSES.

② I DID EXACTLY TWICE AS MANY MIRACLES AS ELIJAH.

③ A GANG OF YOUTHS ONCE MADE FUN OF MY BALD HEAD.

(ANSWER BELOW)

BIBLE QUIZ

WHO, IN JOHN'S GOSPEL, IS THE "SON OF PERDITION"?

JUDAS ISCARIOT (17:12)

PEACOCKS DO NOT LAY EGGS! PEAHENS DO! PEACOCKS ARE THE MALES OF THE PEAFOWL FAMILY.

PRESIDENT ANDREW JOHNSON'S WIFE TAUGHT HIM HOW TO READ AND WRITE.

"COUNTLESS TIMES I HAVE HEARD CHRISTIANS SAY, 'WHY DO I NEED TO STUDY DOCTRINE OR THEOLOGY WHEN ALL I NEED TO KNOW IS JESUS?' MY IMMEDIATE REPLY IS THIS: 'WHO IS JESUS?' AS SOON AS WE BEGIN TO ANSWER THAT QUESTION, WE ARE INVOLVED IN DOCTRINE AND THEOLOGY. NO CHRISTIAN CAN AVOID THEOLOGY. EVERY CHRISTIAN IS A THEOLOGIAN... THE ISSUE... IS WHETHER WE ARE GOING TO BE GOOD THEOLOGIANS OR BAD ONES. A GOOD THEOLOGIAN IS ONE WHO IS INSTRUCTED BY GOD." — J.I. PACKER

ANSWER TO "WHO AM I?" ——— ELISHA

60

AWESOME TRUTH by Eddie Eddings

> "HE WHO CONCEALS HIS SINS DOES NOT PROSPER, BUT WHOEVER CONFESSES AND RENOUNCES THEM FINDS MERCY."
>
> PROVERBS 28:13 (NIV)

WHO AM I?

① I SUFFERED FROM SEVERAL MENTAL BREAKDOWNS AND WAS CONFINED TO AN ASYLUM IN 1721.

② INFLUENCED BY THE PREACHING OF WESLEY, I CAME TO THINK OF MYSELF AS A PUBLIC GUARDIAN OF ENGLAND'S MORALS, CALLING MYSELF "ALEXANDER, THE CORRECTOR."

③ I'M THE AUTHOR OF A FAMOUS CONCORDANCE.

(ANSWER BELOW)

> "I NEVER SAY THAT CIVILIZATION IS GOING TO THE DOGS. I STILL HAVE SOME RESPECT FOR DOGS! MANKIND WITHOUT THE GRACE OF GOD IS DOING THINGS BENEATH THE DIGNITY OF THE BEASTS OF THE FIELD." — VANCE HAVNER

BIBLE QUIZ:

WHAT QUEEN OF ISRAEL PRACTICED WITCHCRAFT?

JEZEBEL (2 KINGS 9:22)

GUESS WHO

INTRODUCED ICE CREAM — AND WAFFLES — AND MACARONI TO THE UNITED STATES.

THOMAS JEFFERSON THAT'S WHO!

ABRAHAM LINCOLN DID NOT HAVE A MIDDLE NAME.

ANSWER TO "WHO AM I?" — ALEXANDER CRUDEN

61

AWESOME TRUTH
by Eddie Eddings

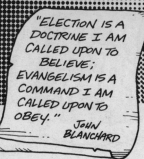

"ELECTION IS A DOCTRINE I AM CALLED UPON TO BELIEVE; EVANGELISM IS A COMMAND I AM CALLED UPON TO OBEY."
... JOHN BLANCHARD

WHO AM I?

① I, FOR ONE, REALLY APPRECIATE A FINE WICKER BASKET.

② I HAD A 40-YEAR POSTGRADUATE COURSE AT GOD'S "UNIVERSITY"— THE DESERT.

③ MICHAEL, THE ARCHANGEL, AND SATAN FOUGHT OVER MY BODY AFTER MY DEATH. (ANSWER BELOW)

THE OSTRICH CAN OUTRUN A RACEHORSE!

BIBLE QUIZ:

WHAT HAPPENS TO THE SEA IN THE WORLD TO COME?

IT DOES NOT EXIST (REVELATION 22:1)

JUST FOR FUN:

AS STRONG AS SAMSON WAS, WHAT WAS THE ONE THING HE COULDN'T HOLD FOR LONG?

HIS BREATH!

"THERE IS A BIG DIFFERENCE BETWEEN EXERCISING ONE'S CRITICAL FACULTY, AND INDULGING IN A CRITICAL SPIRIT. FOR THE FORMER WE THANK GOD AND PRAY TO USE IT REVERENTLY. FROM THE LATTER MAY OUR DEAR LORD SAVE US AND GIVE US INSTEAD A GRACIOUS SYMPATHY."   J. SIDLOW BAXTER

WHEN QUEEN ELIZABETH WAS 18 YEARS OLD SHE WAS A MECHANIC IN THE ENGLISH MILITARY!

ANSWER TO "WHO AM I?" —— MOSES

POWER OF TRUTH

by Eddie Eddings

THINK ABOUT IT:

"I PRAY NOT FOR THE WORLD, BUT FOR THEM WHICH THOU HAST GIVEN ME."

Jesus (John 17:9)

WHO AM I?

① I WAS ONLY SEMI-EDUCATED, NEVER COULD SPELL WELL— BUT FOUNDED A BIBLE INSTITUTE.

② AN EX-PICKPOCKET TAUGHT ME TO PREACH THE LOVE OF GOD.

③ THOUGH RIDICULED AS "CRAZY" FOR MY UNRESTRAINED ZEAL I ADMIT TO ALWAYS BEING "MOODY"! (ANSWER BELOW)

IT'S A NATURAL FACT!!

HONEY IS THE **ONLY** FOOD THAT DOESN'T SPOIL!

THE MIDDLE INITIAL IN HARRY S TRUMAN'S NAME STANDS FOR NOTHING. —WHEN PROPERLY WRITTEN IT IS NOT FOLLOWED BY A PERIOD.

QUOTES

"UPON A LIFE I DID NOT LIVE, UPON A DEATH I DID NOT DIE, I RISK MY WHOLE ETERNITY— AND THE RESURRECTION IS THE WHY."

C.H. SPURGEON

BIBLE QUIZ

DOES THE BIBLE STATE THAT DELILAH CUT SAMSON'S HAIR?

NO! —SEE JUDGES 16:19

ANSWER TO "WHO AM I?" — D.L. MOODY

63

AWESOME TRUTH by Eddie Eddings

THE CHRISTMAS HYMN "**SILENT NIGHT**" WAS SUNG FOR THE FIRST TIME ON THE NIGHT OF DECEMBER 24, 1818. SINCE THEN IT HAS BEEN TRANSLATED INTO **EVERY MAJOR LANGUAGE** OF THE **WORLD!**

SILENT NIGHT

WHO AM I?

① MY GREAT GRANDFATHER WAS ENOCH, WHO ESCAPED DEATH BY BEING TRANSLATED.

② I HAD A GOD-GIVEN TASK THAT MADE ME A LAUGHINGSTOCK, YET I TOILED ON, YEAR AFTER YEAR.

③ GOD CLOSED THE DOOR ON MY PROJECT.

(ANSWER BELOW)

BIBLE QUIZ: WHAT PROPHET WOULD NOT DECLARE HIS PROPHECY UNTIL MUSIC WAS PLAYED?

ELISHA (II KINGS 3:15)

THOMAS JEFFERSON'S TOMBSTONE **OMITS ALL REFERENCE** TO THE FACT THAT HE WAS ONCE THE **PRESIDENT** OF THE UNITED STATES!

JEFFERSON

"AN HONEST BELIEF IN THE **SOVEREIGNTY OF GOD IN SALVATION** WOULD BRING AN **END TO A LOT OF THE NONSENSE** THAT IS GOING ON IN THE CHURCH."

JOHN MacARTHUR, JR.

"OF TWO EVILS, CHOOSE NEITHER." — SPURGEON

ANSWER TO "WHO AM I?" —NOAH

AWESOME TRUTH

by Eddie Eddings

"FOR IT HAS BEEN **GRANTED** TO YOU THAT FOR THE SAKE OF CHRIST YOU SHOULD NOT ONLY **BELIEVE** IN HIM BUT ALSO SUFFER FOR HIS SAKE." PHILLIPIANS 1:29

WHO AM I?

① I WAS FORCED TO SERVE AS A GALLEY SLAVE FOR THE FRENCH FOR NINETEEN MONTHS.

② I LED THE PROTESTANT REFORMATION IN SCOTLAND.

③ I WAS IN DIRECT CONFLICT WITH MARY, QUEEN OF SCOTS. BUT AFTER HER ABDICATION IN 1567 I PREACHED AT THE CORONATION OF HER SON, JAMES VI. (ANSWER BELOW)

GEORGE WASHINGTON WAS FORMALLY ACCORDED THE OFFICIAL TITLE OF "HIS HIGHNESS, THE PRESIDENT OF THE UNITED STATES."

THE PROPER GREETING WAS NOT TO SHAKE HANDS **BUT TO BOW.**

TRUE OR FALSE

ONE OF DAVID'S ANCESTORS WAS A SALMON.

TRUE! (MATT. 1:5) THAT WAS HIS GREAT, GREAT GRANDFATHER'S NAME.

"SIN IS THE DARE OF GOD'S JUSTICE, THE RAPE OF HIS MERCY, THE SLIGHT OF HIS POWER, AND THE CONTEMPT OF HIS LOVE." — John Bunyan

BIBLE QUIZ

WHERE DID ELIJAH FIND ELISHA?

IN A FIELD PLOWING (1 KINGS 19:19)

ANSWER TO "WHO AM I?"— JOHN KNOX

65

AWESOME TOY TRIK
by Eddie Eddings

"THOUGH GOD MAY SUFFER HIS PEOPLE TO FALL INTO SIN, HE WILL NOT SUFFER HIS PEOPLE TO LIE STILL IN SIN."

MATTHEW HENRY

WHO AM I?

① I WAS A COLONIAL AMERICAN MINISTER. MY OLDEST SON WAS NAMED COTTON.

② I WAS PRESIDENT OF HARVARD COLLEGE FROM 1684-1701.

③ I HELPED END EXECUTIONS FOR WITCHCRAFT IN COLONIAL AMERICA. (ANSWER BELOW)

FILL IN THE BLANK

"LOVE NOT _____, LEST THOU COME TO POVERTY."
(PROVERBS 20:13)

ANSWER: SLEEP

ONLY 4 PRESIDENTS OF THE UNITED STATES HAD A SURNAME CONTAINING ONLY 4 LETTERS: CAN YOU NAME THEM?

POLK, TAFT, FORD AND BUSH

GEOGRAPHY LESSON:

HAWAII IS THE STATE FARTHEST SOUTH. ALASKA IS THE STATE FARTHEST NORTH, WEST and EAST!

EDGAR ALLEN POE'S *LAST WORDS WERE* — "LORD HAVE MERCY ON MY POOR SOUL!"

ALASKA'S STATE FLAG WAS DESIGNED BY A CHILD!

ANSWER TO "WHO AM I?" — INCREASE MATHER

66

AWESOME TRUTH

by Eddie Eddings

"IF I COULD HEAR CHRIST PRAYING FOR ME IN THE NEXT ROOM, I WOULD NOT FEAR A MILLION OF ENEMIES. YET THE DISTANCE MAKES NO DIFFERENCE; HE IS PRAYING FOR ME!"

Robert Murray M'Cheyne

WHO AM I?

① SOME HAVE CALLED ME "THE FATHER OF ORTHODOX THEOLOGY" OTHERS "ANTIQUITY'S GREATEST THEOLOGIAN."

② GOD USED A CHILD SINGING "TAKE IT AND READ, TAKE IT AND READ" TO OPEN MY BIBLE AND BE CONVERTED.

③ MY WRITINGS CONTRIBUTED MORE TO THE REVIVAL OF TRUE RELIGION THAN DID THOSE OF ANY OTHER MAN BETWEEN PAUL AND LUTHER.

JAMES BUCHANAN HAS BEEN THE ONLY BACHELOR TO SERVE AS PRESIDENT OF THE UNITED STATES!

ENGLISH POET, BEN JONSON, WAS BURIED IN WESTMINSTER ABBEY— **STANDING UP!**

BUCHANAN

BIBLE QUIZ:

WHAT VERSE IN THE BIBLE REVEALS THAT THE EARTH IS ROUND?

WHERE IN THE BIBLE IS IT REVEALED THAT THIS PLANET IS SUSPENDED IN SPACE?

ISAIAH 40:22

JOB 26:7

ANSWER TO "WHO AM I?"—AUGUSTINE OF HIPPO

67

AWESOME TRUTH

by Eddie Eddings

THERE ARE **HUNDREDS** OF MICROSCOPIC CREATURES CALLED **DEMODI FOLLICULORUM** CRAWLING ON YOUR FACE RIGHT NOW!

WHO AM I?

① I HAD ONE OF THE MOST AMAZING CALLS TO GOD'S SERVICE OF ANY PERSON IN THE BIBLE.

② I MINISTERED BEFORE THE LORD WHILE STILL A CHILD.

③ I ESTABLISHED WHAT IS THOUGHT TO BE THE FIRST SCHOOL OF THE PROPHETS. (ANSWER BELOW)

"PEACE IF POSSIBLE BUT TRUTH AT ANY RATE."

MARTIN LUTHER

TRUE OR FALSE?

THE TEN COMMANDMENTS WERE WRITTEN ON TWO STONE TABLETS USING THE FRONT AND BACK OF EACH.

ANSWER: TRUE! (EXODUS 32:15)

"DID JESUS SATISFY GOD'S JUSTICE ON THE CROSS? OR DO WE SATISFY GOD'S JUSTICE WHEN WE BELIEVE? IF YOUR ANSWER IS 'AT THE CROSS,' THEN YOU BELIEVE THAT EVERYONE FOR WHOM CHRIST DIED IS CLEARED OF ALL CHARGES, BEFORE GOD. IF YOUR ANSWER IS 'WHEN WE BELIEVE,' ONE WONDERS WHO IS THE REAL SAVIOR IN THIS MATTER!"

MICHAEL SCOTT HORTON

ANSWER TO "WHO AM I?" ——— SAMUEL

68

WHO AM I?

by Eddie Eddings

① I BEGAN PRISON FELLOWSHIP IN 1976.

② ONE WORD — "WATERGATE."

③ TWO WORDS — "BORN AGAIN."

(ANSWER BELOW)

IT'S TRUE!

THE **CANARY ISLANDS** WERE NAMED FOR A BREED OF LARGE **DOGS**!

ONE OF THE REASONS **BENJAMIN FRANKLIN** WAS NOT ENTRUSTED BY HIS PEERS WITH THE ASSIGNMENT OF WRITING **THE DECLARATION OF INDEPENDENCE** WAS THAT THEY WERE AFRAID HE MIGHT CONCEAL A **JOKE** IN IT.

BIBLE QUIZ

WHO MOVED THE STONE AT JESUS' TOMB AND THEN SAT ON IT?

AN ANGEL (MATTHEW 28:2)

"CALVIN

DID NOT INVENT A NEW TEACHING ANY MORE THAN COLUMBUS INVENTED AMERICA OR NEWTON THE LAW OF GRAVITY." —— EDWIN PALMER

"HOW BLESSED IS THE MAN TO WHOM THE LORD DOES NOT IMPUTE INIQUITY."

PSALM 32:2

ANSWER TO "WHO AM I?" — CHUCK COLSON

69

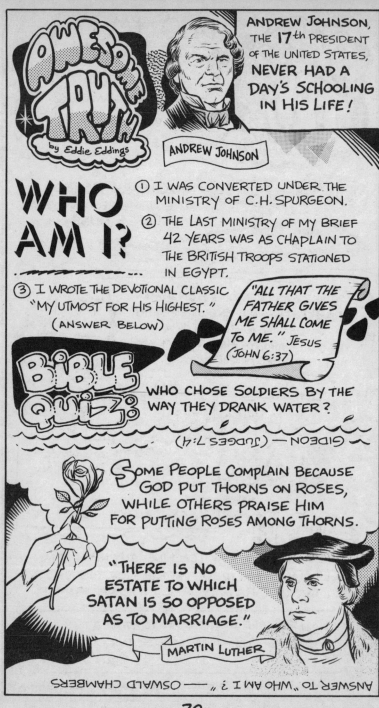

AWESOME TRUTH by Eddie Eddings

ANDREW JOHNSON, THE 17th PRESIDENT OF THE UNITED STATES, NEVER HAD A DAY'S SCHOOLING IN HIS LIFE!

ANDREW JOHNSON

WHO AM I?

① I WAS CONVERTED UNDER THE MINISTRY OF C.H. SPURGEON.

② THE LAST MINISTRY OF MY BRIEF 42 YEARS WAS AS CHAPLAIN TO THE BRITISH TROOPS STATIONED IN EGYPT.

③ I WROTE THE DEVOTIONAL CLASSIC "MY UTMOST FOR HIS HIGHEST." (ANSWER BELOW)

"ALL THAT THE FATHER GIVES ME SHALL COME TO ME." JESUS (JOHN 6:37)

BIBLE QUIZ

WHO CHOSE SOLDIERS BY THE WAY THEY DRANK WATER?

GIDEON — (JUDGES 7:4)

SOME PEOPLE COMPLAIN BECAUSE GOD PUT THORNS ON ROSES, WHILE OTHERS PRAISE HIM FOR PUTTING ROSES AMONG THORNS.

"THERE IS NO ESTATE TO WHICH SATAN IS SO OPPOSED AS TO MARRIAGE."

MARTIN LUTHER

ANSWER TO "WHO AM I?" — OSWALD CHAMBERS

70

AWESOME TRUTH

by Eddie Eddings

"ANYONE CAN DEVISE A PLAN BY WHICH GOOD PEOPLE GO TO HEAVEN. ONLY GOD CAN DEVISE A PLAN WHEREBY SINNERS, WHO ARE HIS ENEMIES, CAN GO TO HEAVEN."

Lewis Sperry Chafer

WHO AM I?

① MY FAIR AND JUST TREATMENT OF THE INDIANS SET THE PATTERN FOR PENNSYLVANIA'S COLONIAL HISTORY.

② I AM AN ENGLISH QUAKER MISSIONARY WHO STUDIED LAW IN LONDON.

③ MY FINEST ACCOMPLISHMENT WAS THE FOUNDING OF PENNSYLVANIA AS A REFUGE FOR RELIGIOUS DISSENTERS.

 THE BLACK BOX (ANSWER BELOW)

OR FLIGHT DATA RECORDER ON AN AIRPLANE IS **ORANGE!**

IT IS CALLED A BLACK BOX BECAUSE IT IS SEALED. IT IS ORANGE TO MAKE IT EASIER TO FIND IN CASE OF AN ACCIDENT.

BIBLE QUIZ:
WHO WAS RELEASED FROM PRISON BY AN ANGEL?
- - - - - - - - - -
(ACTS 12:6-9)
PETER

A.W. TOZER

"NO MAN HAS ANY RIGHT TO PICK AND CHOOSE AMONG REVEALED TRUTHS."

"TRUTH ENGAGES THE CITADEL OF THE HUMAN HEART AND IS NOT SATISFIED UNTIL IT HAS CONQUERED EVERYTHING THERE."

ANSWER TO "WHO AM I?" ——— WILLIAM PENN

AWESOME TRUTH
by Eddie Eddings

BIBLE VERSE TO PONDER:

"THE LORD HATH MADE **ALL THINGS** FOR HIMSELF: YEA, EVEN THE **WICKED** FOR THE DAY OF EVIL."

PROVERBS 16:4

Who Am I?

① A KING SOUGHT TO SLAY ME WHILE I WAS A BABY.

② I WAS SAVED BY HIDING IN EGYPT

③ I AM THE MEEKEST OF MEN.

(ANSWER BELOW)

THE **19th** PRESIDENT OF THE UNITED STATES, **RUTHERFORD HAYES,** HELD MORNING PRAYER READINGS EVERY DAY AFTER BREAKFAST. EVERY SUNDAY NIGHT HE CONDUCTED HYMN-SINGING SESSIONS IN THE WHITE HOUSE.

NO PRESIDENT of the U.S. WAS AN ONLY CHILD.

"WE MUST **BE SURE** THAT OUR CONCEPT OF GOD INCLUDES **ALL** THAT THE BIBLE TEACHES ABOUT HIM."

"IN ANSWER TO THE QUESTION— HOW CAN THE TRINITY EXIST?— I RESPOND, **WHY NOT**?"

R.C. SPROUL

ANSWER TO "WHO AM I?" — MOSES

AWESOME TRUTH by Eddie Eddings

IN ESSENTIALS **UNITY**, IN UNCERTAINTIES **FREEDOM**, IN ALL THINGS **LOVE**.

WHO AM I?

① NOTHING IS KNOWN OF MY PARENTS, BUT I AM ONE OF THE MOST UNIQUE AND DRAMATIC CHARACTERS OF BIBLE HISTORY.

② I TALKED WITH CHRIST AND MOSES ON A CERTAIN DAY.

③ I AM A PROTOTYPE OF JOHN THE BAPTIST.

(ANSWER BELOW)

"ALWAYS AND EVERYWHERE THE SERVANTS OF CHRIST ARE UNDER ORDER TO EVANGELIZE."

J. I. PACKER

IT TOOK 70,000 LABORERS, 80,000 STONE CUTTERS, and 3,600 OVERSEERS TO BUILD THE TEMPLE.

(2 CHRONICLES 2:1-2)

BIBLE QUIZ

WHO COMMANDED: "SEARCH THE SCRIPTURES"?

ANSWER: CHRIST (JOHN 5:39)

ANSWER TO "WHO AM I?" ———— ELIJAH

73

AWESOME TRUTH
by Eddie Eddings

"THE CHURCH NEEDS TIME TO TUNE UP. WE ARE SO BUSY BUILDING A BIGGER ORCHESTRA THAT WE CANNOT STOP TO TUNE OUR INSTRUMENTS."

Vance Havner

WHO AM I?

① MY BIBLICAL BIOGRAPHY DIDN'T EVEN BEGIN UNTIL I WAS 75.

② I FIRST HEARD GOD'S PROMISE OF REAL ESTATE AND CHILDREN BEFORE I LEFT MY HOMETOWN.

③ I WAS CALLED "GOD'S FRIEND" IN JAMES 2:23. (ANSWER BELOW)

"THE BIBLE DOES NOT TEACH THE TYPE OF SALVATION WHICH SAYS, COME TO CHRIST, BELIEVE IN HIM, AND ALL WILL BE WELL; YOU WILL WALK DOWN THE ROAD WITH A BRIGHT STEP AND EVERYTHING WILL BE PERFECT EVER AFTERWARDS. ON THE CONTRARY THE SCRIPTURE WARNS US THAT WE ARE ENTERING A LIFE IN WHICH WE HAVE TO PUT ON 'THE WHOLE ARMOUR OF GOD.'"

D.M. LLOYD-JONES

LONDON BRIDGE IS NOW LOCATED IN ARIZONA

THE BIBLE AMONG BOOKS IS WHAT CHRIST IS AMONG MEN.

BIBLE QUIZ:
WHO ADVISED HER HUSBAND TO STEAL A VINEYARD?
- - - - - - - - - - -
(1 KINGS 21:15) JEZEBEL

THE HAWAIIAN ALPHABET HAS ONLY 12 LETTERS!

ANSWER TO "WHO AM I?" — ABRAHAM

74

AWESOME TRUTH
by Eddie Eddings

" I HAVE MORE TROUBLE WITH D.L. MOODY THAN WITH ANY MAN I EVER MET. "

D.L. MOODY

WHO AM I.?

① IN 1943, I BECAME THE FIRST EVANGELIST OF THE NEWLY FOUNDED YOUTH FOR CHRIST.

② IN 1948, WHILE PRESIDENT OF NORTHWESTERN COLLEGE IN MINNEAPOLIS, I ACQUIRED NATIONAL FAME THROUGH MY LOS ANGELES CRUSADE.

③ MY TEAM INCLUDED CLIFF BARROWS AND GEORGE BEVERLY SHEA.

(ANSWER BELOW)

" SINCE THE BIBLE TEACHES THAT LIFE IN THE WOMB IS HUMAN LIFE, ONE CANNOT ACCEPT ABORTION WITHOUT DENYING THE AUTHORITY AND TRUTH OF SCRIPTURE IN PRACTICE. "

FRANCIS SCHAEFFER

AARON BURR, VICE-PRESIDENT UNDER THOMAS JEFFERSON, WAS THE GRANDSON OF THE REVEREND JONATHAN EDWARDS.

BIBLE QUIZ:

CONCERNING WHAT MAN DID PAUL SAY, " HE DID ME MUCH EVIL"?

ALEXANDER, THE COPPERSMITH (2 TIMOTHY 4:14)

ANSWER TO "WHO AM I ?" ——— BILLY GRAHAM

75

AWESOME TRUTH
by Eddie Eddings

BIBLE QUIZ:
WHO SAW A VISION OF A VALLEY OF DRY BONES?
EZEKIEL

WHO AM I?

① DURING MY FIRST TERM IN COLLEGE I PLAYED CLARINET IN A JAZZ BAND CALLED "THE OXFORD BANDITS."

② I WAS ASSOCIATED WITH THE REVIVAL OF REFORMED THEOLOGY WHICH DR. MARTYN LLOYD-JONES PIONEERED IN BRITAIN.

③ MY MOST POPULAR BOOK, "KNOWING GOD," WAS FIRST PUBLISHED IN 1973.   (ANSWER BELOW)

THE YOUNGEST PRESIDENT EVER TO HOLD OFFICE WAS THEODORE ROOSEVELT.

HE WROTE 30 BOOKS, 3,000 ARTICLES, AND 150,000 LETTERS.

THEODORE ROOSEVELT WORE A RING CONTAINING A LOCK OF HAIR FROM LINCOLN'S HEAD!

"EVERYONE SAYS FORGIVENESS IS A LOVELY IDEA UNTIL HE HAS SOMETHING TO FORGIVE."
C.S. Lewis

A SURE THING:

ROMANS 8:30

"AND THOSE WHOM HE PREDESTINED, HE ALSO CALLED; AND THOSE WHOM HE CALLED, HE ALSO JUSTIFIED; AND THOSE WHOM HE JUSTIFIED, HE ALSO GLORIFIED."

ANSWER TO "WHO AM I?" —— J.I. PACKER

76

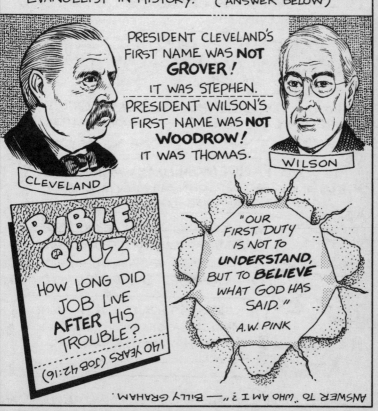

AWESOME TRUTH by Eddie Eddings

"RACE PREJUDICE IS AS THOROUGH A DENIAL OF THE CHRISTIAN GOD AS ATHEISM, AND A FAR MORE COMMON FORM OF APOSTASY."

— HARRY EMERSON FOSDICK

WHO AM I?

① MORE BOOKS HAVE BEEN WRITTEN OF ME THAN ANYONE WHO EVER LIVED.

② IF EVERY ONE OF THE THINGS I DID WERE WRITTEN DOWN, EVEN THE WHOLE WORLD WOULD NOT HAVE ROOM FOR THE BOOKS.

③ I AM THE AUTHOR OF SALVATION AS MENTIONED IN HEBREWS 2:10. (ANSWER BELOW)

BIBLE QUIZ

WHAT OLD TESTAMENT BOOK DOES JESUS QUOTE MORE THAN ANY OTHER? — DEUTERONOMY

THE WORD "PANDEMONIUM" WAS INVENTED BY THE ENGLISH POET JOHN MILTON (1608-1674) AUTHOR OF "PARADISE LOST."

THE ECCENTRIC JOHN ("JOHNNY APPLESEED") CHAPMAN PREACHED THE HERETICAL TEACHINGS OF SWEDISH MYSTIC EMANUEL SWEDENBORG!

"THE KING'S HEART IS IN THE HAND OF THE LORD, AS THE RIVERS OF WATER: HE TURNETH IT WHITHERSOEVER HE WILL." — PROVERBS 21:1

ANSWER TO "WHO AM I?" — THE LORD JESUS CHRIST

by Eddie Eddings

"HE PERMITS, FOR REASONS KNOWN ONLY TO HIMSELF, PEOPLE TO ACT CONTRARY TO AND IN DEFIANCE OF HIS **REVEALED WILL.** BUT [GOD] NEVER PERMITS THEM TO ACT CONTRARY TO HIS **SOVEREIGN WILL.**"

JERRY BRIDGES

① I WROTE "THE SONG OF HIAWATHA" IN 1855 AND "PAUL REVERE'S RIDE" IN 1860.

② THE TRAGIC DEATH OF MY WIFE IN A FIRE TURNED ME TO WRITING MORE SPIRITUAL TOPICS SUCH AS THE ENGLISH TRANSLATION OF DANTE'S DIVINE COMEDY.

③ I ALSO PENNED THE CHRISTMAS HYMN "I HEARD THE BELLS ON CHRISTMAS DAY." _____ (ANSWER BELOW)

The **TEDDY BEAR** WAS NAMED IN PRESIDENT THEODORE ROOSEVELT'S HONOR!

BIBLE QUIZ: WHO WANTED TO BUY THE POWER OF THE HOLY SPIRIT?
- - - - - - - - - - - - -
(ACTS 8:18-19)
SIMON the SORCERER

IN HIS FAMOUS AND PROFOUND WORK, THE "**HISTORY OF CIVILIZATION,**" BUCKLE, HIMSELF THE ADHERENT OF NO RELIGIOUS CREED, ADMITTED THIS **HISTORICAL FACT**: "THE MOST PROFOUND THINKERS HAVE BEEN ON THE **CALVINISTIC** SIDE; AND IT IS INTERESTING TO OBSERVE THAT THIS SUPERIORITY OF THOUGHT ON THE PART OF THE CALVINISTS EXISTED FROM THE BEGINNING."

THOMAS JEFFERSON RELAXED BY PLAYING THE FIDDLE.

ANSWER TO "WHO AM I?"—HENRY WADSWORTH LONGFELLOW

AWESOME TRUTH
by Eddie Eddings

"A **DOG** BARKS WHEN HIS MASTER IS ATTACKED. I WOULD BE A **COWARD** IF I SAW THAT GOD'S TRUTH IS ATTACKED AND YET WOULD **REMAIN SILENT**, WITHOUT GIVING ANY SOUND."

--- JOHN CALVIN

WHO AM I?

① YES, I SMOKED CIGARS, BUT IN MY TIME THE PRACTICE WAS BELIEVED TO BE BENEFICIAL TO ONE'S HEALTH.

② I KEPT A HIVE OF BEES AT WESTWOOD AND TOOK DELIGHT IN CARING FOR THEM WHEN I HAD TIME.

③ ONE OF THE GREAT CONTROVERSIES I WAS INVOLVED IN WAS KNOWN AS THE "DOWN-GRADE CONTROVERSY". (ANSWER BELOW)

MEMORY VERSE

"FOR AS THE FATHER RAISES THE DEAD AND GIVES THEM LIFE, SO ALSO THE SON GIVES LIFE TO WHOM HE WILL."

JOHN 5:21

GEORGE WASHINGTON,
THE **FATHER** OF HIS COUNTRY, **WAS NEVER A FATHER!** HE ADOPTED THE TWO CHILDREN OF MARTHA CUSTIS.

BIBLE QUIZ

WHAT PROPHET WAS COMMANDED TO LIE FOR **390** DAYS UPON HIS LEFT SIDE, AND **40** DAYS UPON HIS RIGHT? ...... (EZEKIEL 4:4-6) EZEKIEL

ANSWER TO "WHO AM I?" —— CHARLES HADDON SPURGEON

80

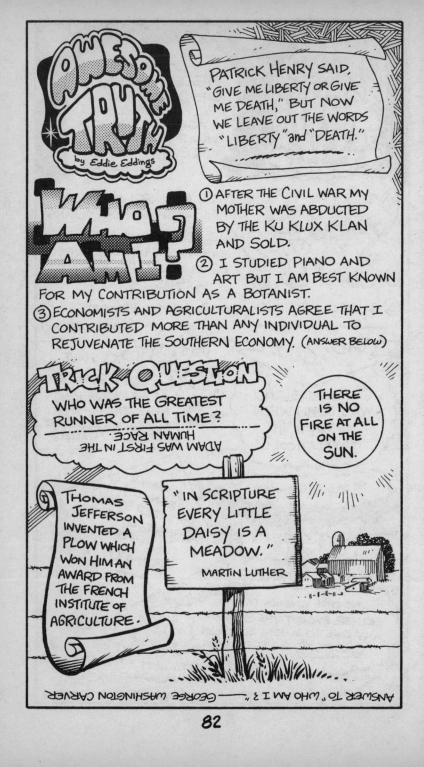

AWESOME TRUTH by Eddie Eddings

PATRICK HENRY SAID, "GIVE ME LIBERTY OR GIVE ME DEATH," BUT NOW WE LEAVE OUT THE WORDS "LIBERTY" and "DEATH."

WHO AM I?

① AFTER THE CIVIL WAR MY MOTHER WAS ABDUCTED BY THE KU KLUX KLAN AND SOLD.

② I STUDIED PIANO AND ART BUT I AM BEST KNOWN FOR MY CONTRIBUTION AS A BOTANIST.

③ ECONOMISTS AND AGRICULTURALISTS AGREE THAT I CONTRIBUTED MORE THAN ANY INDIVIDUAL TO REJUVENATE THE SOUTHERN ECONOMY. (ANSWER BELOW)

TRICK QUESTION

WHO WAS THE GREATEST RUNNER OF ALL TIME?

ADAM WAS FIRST IN THE HUMAN RACE.

THERE IS NO FIRE AT ALL ON THE SUN.

THOMAS JEFFERSON INVENTED A PLOW WHICH WON HIM AN AWARD FROM THE FRENCH INSTITUTE OF AGRICULTURE.

"IN SCRIPTURE EVERY LITTLE DAISY IS A MEADOW." MARTIN LUTHER

ANSWER TO "WHO AM I?" — GEORGE WASHINGTON CARVER

82

AWESOME TRUTH by Eddie Eddings

"THE WICKED SHALL DRINK A SEA OF WRATH, BUT NOT ONE DROP OF INJUSTICE."

THOMAS WATSON

WHO AM I?

① FOR 24 YEARS I RULED AS A JUDGE OVER ISRAEL.

② MY WALK ON THE WILD SIDE LED ME TO MY DEATH.

③ MY HAIR WAS AN OUTWARD SYMBOL OF MY INWARD COMMITTMENT TO GOD. (ANSWER BELOW)

IT'S A NATURAL FACT:

LIGHTNING IS MORE LIKELY THAN NOT TO **STRIKE TWICE IN THE SAME PLACE!** LIKE ALL ELECTRIC DISCHARGES, IT FOLLOWS THE PATH OF LEAST RESISTANCE.

"YOU **OUGHT** TO SAY, 'IF IT BE THE LORD'S WILL, WE WILL LIVE AND DO THIS OR THAT!'" (JAMES 4:15)

BIBLE QUIZ

Jimmy Carter IS THE **FIRST** PRESIDENT TO HAVE BEEN BORN IN A **HOSPITAL**!

WHAT VERSE OF SCRIPTURE REVEALS THE GREAT SECRET OF PHYSICAL LIFE?

"THE LIFE OF THE FLESH IS IN THE BLOOD." (LEVITICUS 17:11)

ANSWER TO "WHO AM I?" ——— SAMSON

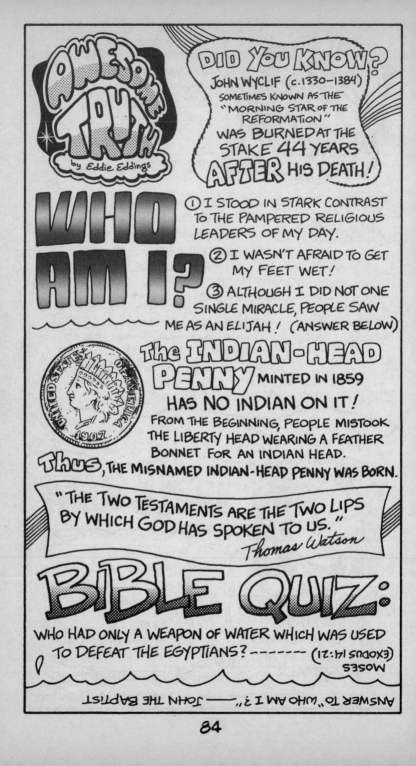

AWESOME TRUTH
by Eddie Eddings

DID YOU KNOW?

JOHN WYCLIF (c. 1330–1384) SOMETIMES KNOWN AS THE "MORNING STAR OF THE REFORMATION" WAS BURNED AT THE STAKE 44 YEARS **AFTER** HIS DEATH!

WHO AM I?

① I STOOD IN STARK CONTRAST TO THE PAMPERED RELIGIOUS LEADERS OF MY DAY.

② I WASN'T AFRAID TO GET MY FEET WET!

③ ALTHOUGH I DID NOT ONE SINGLE MIRACLE, PEOPLE SAW ME AS AN ELIJAH! (ANSWER BELOW)

The INDIAN-HEAD PENNY MINTED IN 1859 HAS NO INDIAN ON IT!

FROM THE BEGINNING, PEOPLE MISTOOK THE LIBERTY HEAD WEARING A FEATHER BONNET FOR AN INDIAN HEAD.

Thus, THE MISNAMED INDIAN-HEAD PENNY WAS BORN.

"THE TWO TESTAMENTS ARE THE TWO LIPS BY WHICH GOD HAS SPOKEN TO US."
Thomas Watson

BIBLE QUIZ:

WHO HAD ONLY A WEAPON OF WATER WHICH WAS USED TO DEFEAT THE EGYPTIANS? ------- (EXODUS 14:21)
MOSES

ANSWER TO "WHO AM I?" —— JOHN THE BAPTIST

84

AWESOME TRUTH by Eddie Eddings

HISTORY IS HIS STORY!

EVERY UNITED STATES PRESIDENT HAS WORN EYEGLASSES!

WHO AM I?

① I AM THE MOST INFLUENTIAL AMERICAN PRESBYTERIAN THEOLOGIAN OF THE NINETEENTH CENTURY.

② I WAS BEST KNOWN IN MY DAY AS A POLEMICIST AND AS A POPULAR EXPONENT OF CALVINISTIC SPIRITUALITY.

③ I AM THE AUTHOR OF A SYSTEMATIC THEOLOGY AND MAJOR COMMENTARIES ON ROMANS, EPHESIANS, AND FIRST AND SECOND CORINTHIANS. (ANSWER BELOW)

JOHN HANCOCK WAS THE ONLY ONE OF THE 56 SIGNERS OF THE DECLARATION OF INDEPENDENCE WHO ACTUALLY SIGNED IT ON JULY 4th!

BIBLE QUIZ:

WHAT MAN ATE A LITTLE BOOK—IN HIS MOUTH IT WAS SWEET, BUT AFTERWARD IT BECAME BITTER? -----

JOHN (REVELATION 10:10)

BOOKS ARE TEACHERS / WHO / INSTRUCT US / WITHOUT ANGER / IF YOU APPROACH THEM / They are Not / ASLEEP / IF YOU SEEK THEM / THEY DO NOT HIDE / IF YOU BLUNDER / THEY DO NOT SCOLD / IF YOU ARE IGNORANT / THEY DO NOT LAUGH AT YOU / THEY ARE READY / TO REPEAT THEIR LESSON / AS OFTEN AS WE PLEASE

ANSWER TO "WHO AM I?": ——— CHARLES HODGE

by Eddie Eddings

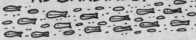

IT'S A FACT!

THERE IS NO SUCH FISH AS SARDINES!

"SARDINE" IS A GENERIC NAME FOR MANY DIFFERENT KINDS OF SMALL FISH!

① MY "FRUIT OF THE GROUND" OFFERING GAVE ME A "SOUR-GRAPES" ATTITUDE.

② JEALOUSY OVER MY BROTHER'S OFFERING BORE BITTER FRUIT.

③ I WAS THE FIRST TO COMMIT FIRST-DEGREE MURDER.

(ANSWER BELOW)

BIBLE QUIZ:

NAME TWO KINGS WHO COULD NOT INTERPRET THEIR OWN DREAMS.

"INSIDE THE WILL OF GOD THERE IS NO FAILURE.

OUTSIDE THE WILL OF GOD THERE IS NO SUCCESS."

Benard Edinger

ANSWER: PHARAOH and NEBUCHADNEZZAR

"ALL THE DAYS ORDAINED FOR ME WERE WRITTEN IN YOUR BOOK BEFORE ONE OF THEM CAME TO BE."

PSALM 139:16 NIV

ANSWER TO "WHO AM I?" ——— CAIN

AWESOME TRUTH

by Eddie Eddings

"IT IS IMPOSSIBLE TO SAVE A LIFE FROM BURNING AND AVOID THE HEAT OF THE FIRE."

MARY S. WOOD

WHO AM I?

① I WAS THE CAPTAIN OF THE SYRIAN ARMY.

② I WAS ALSO A LEPER. ③ I HAD A YOUNG JEWISH SLAVE GIRL WHO TOLD ME ABOUT A PROPHET WHO COULD CURE ME.

(ANSWER BELOW)

WILLIAM HENRY HARRISON, 9th PRESIDENT OF THE UNITED STATES, WAS THE **FIRST** TO DIE IN OFFICE AFTER SERVING ONLY **32** DAYS!

HE WAS THE SON OF A SIGNER OF THE DECLARATION OF INDEPENDENCE AND THE GRANDFATHER OF A PRESIDENT!

BIBLE QUIZ

WHO WAS THE FATHER OF JOHN THE BAPTIST?

(ZACHARIAS) (LUKE 1:59-63)

THOMAS EDISON INVENTED WAX PAPER!

"FOR IN CHRIST ALL THE FULLNESS OF THE DEITY LIVE IN BODILY FORM." COLOSSIANS 2:9

"OUR GOD IS A MISSIONARY GOD." WILLIAM J.C. WHITE

ANSWER TO "WHO AM I?"——NAAMAN

AWESOME TRUTH by Eddie Eddings

BIBLE QUIZ:

By the use of what word does the Bible describe an atheist? — The "Fool." Psalm 14:1

Who Am I?

① My middle name is "CASH" and I built my business on "GOLDEN RULE" ethics.

② I used to write a column for "CHRISTIAN HERALD" magazine entitled "LINES OF A LAYMAN."

③ My department store chain is an American institution with some 1400 stores across every state. (ANSWER BELOW)

WE MUST DO GOD'S WORK IN GOD'S WAY!

A chip on the shoulder indicates there is wood higher up.

ABRAHAM LINCOLN

was clean-shaven until his 51ST year! Shortly after his election to the presidency he began to grow a beard at the suggestion of an eleven year old girl who told him whiskers would "look a great deal better for you for your face is so thin."

"If you were arrested for being a Christian would there be enough evidence to convict you?"

DAVID OTIS FULLER

ANSWER TO "WHO AM I?" — J.C. PENNY

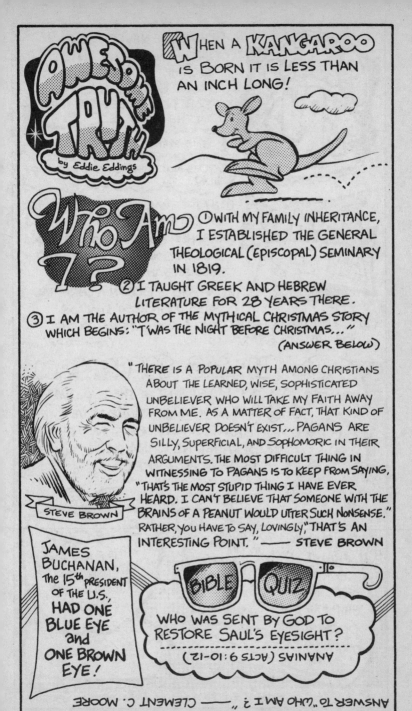

AWESOME TRUTH by Eddie Eddings

WHEN A **KANGAROO** IS BORN IT IS LESS THAN AN INCH LONG!

Who Am I?

① WITH MY FAMILY INHERITANCE, I ESTABLISHED THE GENERAL THEOLOGICAL (EPISCOPAL) SEMINARY IN 1819.

② I TAUGHT GREEK AND HEBREW LITERATURE FOR 28 YEARS THERE.

③ I AM THE AUTHOR OF THE MYTHICAL CHRISTMAS STORY WHICH BEGINS: "T'WAS THE NIGHT BEFORE CHRISTMAS..."

(ANSWER BELOW)

STEVE BROWN

"THERE IS A POPULAR MYTH AMONG CHRISTIANS ABOUT THE LEARNED, WISE, SOPHISTICATED UNBELIEVER WHO WILL TAKE MY FAITH AWAY FROM ME. AS A MATTER OF FACT, THAT KIND OF UNBELIEVER DOESN'T EXIST... PAGANS ARE SILLY, SUPERFICIAL, AND SOPHOMORIC IN THEIR ARGUMENTS. THE MOST DIFFICULT THING IN WITNESSING TO PAGANS IS TO KEEP FROM SAYING, "THAT'S THE MOST STUPID THING I HAVE EVER HEARD. I CAN'T BELIEVE THAT SOMEONE WITH THE BRAINS OF A PEANUT WOULD UTTER SUCH NONSENSE." RATHER, YOU HAVE TO SAY, LOVINGLY, "THAT'S AN INTERESTING POINT." —— STEVE BROWN

JAMES BUCHANAN, THE 15th PRESIDENT OF THE U.S. HAD ONE BLUE EYE AND ONE BROWN EYE!

BIBLE QUIZ

WHO WAS SENT BY GOD TO RESTORE SAUL'S EYESIGHT?

- - - - - - - - - - - -

ANANIAS (ACTS 9:10-12)

ANSWER TO "WHO AM I?" —— CLEMENT C. MOORE

by Eddie Eddings

THERE HAS **NEVER** BEEN A PERSON WHO HAS **WANTED** TO COME TO CHRIST, WHO HAS FOUND GOD'S DECREE OF ELECTION TO BE A BARRIER IN THE WAY!

IT IS POINTLESS TO PRAY FOR THE CONVERSION OF A SOUL, IF GOD IS NOT SOVEREIGN IN REDEMPTION.

WHO AM I?

① BY THE TIME OF MY DEATH IN 1912, I HAD TRAVELED 5 MILLION MILES, PREACHED 60,000 SERMONS AND DRAWN SOME 16,000 ENLISTED SOLDIERS INTO MY ARMY.

② IN 1865 I BEGAN A CHRISTIAN MISSION IN EAST LONDON.

③ I WAS THE FOUNDER AND FIRST GENERAL OF THE SALVATION ARMY.

(ANSWER BELOW)

THOMAS JEFFERSON, 3RD PRESIDENT OF THE U.S., WAS A GIFTED INVENTOR WHO NEVER PATENTED ANY OF HIS INVENTIONS, BECAUSE HE WANTED THE PEOPLE TO HAVE FREE USE OF THEM.

REVELATION 3:20 SPEAKS OF CHRIST KNOCKING ON THE DOOR OF CHURCH MEMBERS OFFERING RESTORED FELLOWSHIP AND **NOT** AT THE DOOR OF UNBELIEVERS OFFERING THEM ETERNAL LIFE!

BIBLE QUIZ: IS THE FORBIDDEN FRUIT IDENTIFIED AS AN APPLE IN THE BIBLE?

ANSWER: NO!

ANSWER TO "WHO AM I?" —— WILLIAM BOOTH

AWESOME TRUTH
by Eddie Eddings

"CALVINISTIC THEOLOGY IS THE GREATEST SUBJECT THAT HAS EVER EXERCISED THE MIND OF MAN."
— LORAINE BOETTNER

WHO AM I?

① I CALLED THE RELIGIOUS LEADERS IN MY DAY A "BUNCH OF SNAKES!"

② YOU COULD SAY I PREFERRED NATURAL FOODS.

③ JESUS SAID OF ME, "AMONG THOSE BORN OF WOMEN THERE HAS NOT ARISEN ANYONE GREATER!"

(ANSWER BELOW)

UMBRELLAS WERE INVENTED NOT TO KEEP OFF THE RAIN, BUT TO KEEP THE SUN OFF. "UMBRELLA" IS LATIN FOR "LITTLE SHADED AREA."

BIBLE QUIZ: HOW MANY BOOKS OF THE BIBLE DID JAMES WRITE?

ANSWER: ONE

GERALD FORD, 38th PRESIDENT OF THE U.S., WAS BORN WITH THE NAME... LESLIE LYNCH KING, JR.

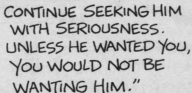
C.S. LEWIS SAID "CONTINUE SEEKING HIM WITH SERIOUSNESS. UNLESS HE WANTED YOU, YOU WOULD NOT BE WANTING HIM."

ANSWER TO "WHO AM I?" ——— JOHN THE BAPTIST

AWESOME TRUTH
by Eddie Eddings

"GOD LOVETH THE LOWEST SAINT MORE THAN THE HIGHEST ANGEL LOVETH GOD."

VALDESSO

WHO AM I?

① I WAS THE FIRST BAPTIST TO DEVELOP A COMPLETE SYSTEMATIC THEOLOGY and THE FIRST BAPTIST TO WRITE A VERSE-BY-VERSE COMMENTARY ON THE ENTIRE BIBLE.

② BY THE AGE OF TEN I HAD READ THROUGH THE ENTIRE GREEK NEW TESTAMENT. I TAUGHT MYSELF HEBREW.

③ MY MAJOR DEFENSE OF CALVINISM, "THE CAUSE OF GOD AND TRUTH," FIRST PUBLISHED IN THE EARLY EIGHTEENTH CENTURY IS STILL AVAILABLE TODAY. (ANSWER BELOW)

BIBLE QUIZ

WHO "SUFFERED MANY THINGS" IN A DREAM BECAUSE OF JESUS?

(PILATE'S WIFE) (MATTHEW 27:19)

EVERY PERSON LIVES IN ONE OF TWO TENTS:

CON-TENT OR DISCON-TENT

IN WHICH DO **YOU** LIVE?

CHARLES STANLEY

"NOWHERE DOES SCRIPTURE TEACH THAT GOD HAS PURPOSED THAT EVERY MAN AND WOMAN BE SAVED."

ANSWER TO "WHO AM I?" ——— JOHN GILL

92

AWESOME TRUTH by Eddie Eddings

"NOT **FREE**-WILL BUT **SELF**-WILL WOULD MORE APPROPRIATELY DESCRIBE MAN'S CONDITION SINCE THE FALL."
— LORAINE BOETTNER

WHO AM I?

① I WAS A DEVOTED MEMBER OF THE PROTESTANT EPISCOPAL CHURCH, AND TAUGHT BIBLE CLASSES IN AND AROUND WASHINGTON, D.C.

② I WAS AMONG THE ORGANIZERS OF THE DOMESTIC AND FOREIGN MISSIONARY SOCIETY, FOUNDED IN 1820.

③ I WROTE AMERICA'S NATIONAL ANTHEM. (ANSWER BELOW)

GROVER CLEVELAND IS THE **ONLY** PRESIDENT TO HAVE BEEN MARRIED IN THE WHITE HOUSE!

"GOD NEVER REPENTS OF HIS ELECTING LOVE."
— Thomas Watson

WINSTON CHURCHILL WAS BORN IN A LADIES' CLOAKROOM!

BIBLE QUIZ

WHAT MAN FOR HIS OWN PROTECTION IN A FOREIGN COUNTRY PRETENDED THAT HE WAS INSANE?

DAVID (1 SAMUEL 21)

"NEVER THINK TO FIND HONEY IN THE POT WHEN GOD WRITES POISON ON ITS COVER."
— WILLIAM GURNALL

ANSWER TO "WHO AM I?" — FRANCIS SCOTT KEY

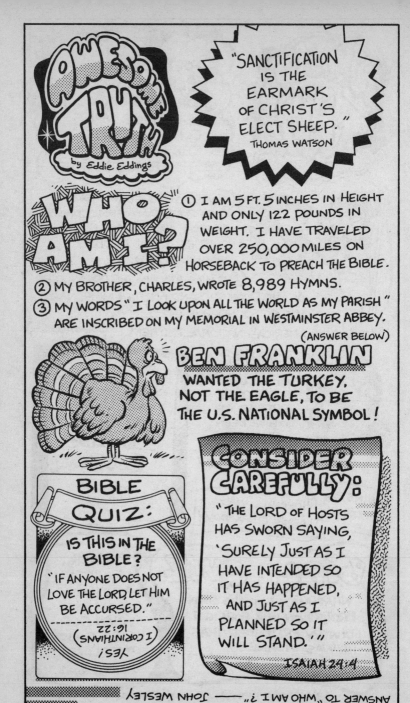

AWESOME TRUTH
by Eddie Eddings

"SANCTIFICATION IS THE EARMARK OF CHRIST'S ELECT SHEEP."
THOMAS WATSON

WHO AM I?

① I AM 5 FT. 5 INCHES IN HEIGHT AND ONLY 122 POUNDS IN WEIGHT. I HAVE TRAVELED OVER 250,000 MILES ON HORSEBACK TO PREACH THE BIBLE.

② MY BROTHER, CHARLES, WROTE 8,989 HYMNS.

③ MY WORDS "I LOOK UPON ALL THE WORLD AS MY PARISH" ARE INSCRIBED ON MY MEMORIAL IN WESTMINSTER ABBEY.

(ANSWER BELOW)

BEN FRANKLIN WANTED THE TURKEY, NOT THE EAGLE, TO BE THE U.S. NATIONAL SYMBOL!

BIBLE QUIZ:

IS THIS IN THE BIBLE?

"IF ANYONE DOES NOT LOVE THE LORD LET HIM BE ACCURSED."

YES! (I CORINTHIANS 16:22)

CONSIDER CAREFULLY:

"THE LORD OF HOSTS HAS SWORN SAYING, 'SURELY JUST AS I HAVE INTENDED SO IT HAS HAPPENED, AND JUST AS I PLANNED SO IT WILL STAND.'"

ISAIAH 24:4

ANSWER TO "WHO AM I?" —— JOHN WESLEY

AWESOME TRUTH
by Eddie Eddings

"THE STRENGTH OF A COUNTRY IS THE STRENGTH OF ITS **RELIGIOUS CONVICTIONS.**"

— CALVIN COOLIDGE
30th PRESIDENT
OF THE UNITED STATES

WHO AM I?

① WHEN IT WAS DISCOVERED THAT I WAS INVOLVED IN AN ANTI-NAZI MILITARY INTELLIGENCE OPERATION, HITLER ORDERED MY EXECUTION.

② I, A 39 YEAR OLD GERMAN PASTOR, AFTER LENGTHY INTERROGATIONS BY THE GESTAPO, WENT TO THE GALLOWS ON APRIL 5, 1945.

③ MY BOOK "THE COST OF DISCIPLESHIP" HAS LEFT AN INDELIBLE IMPRINT ON THE THINKING OF MANY CHRISTIANS.

(ANSWER BELOW)

THINK IT OVER

"...AND AS MANY AS WERE **ORDAINED TO ETERNAL LIFE** BELIEVED."

(ACTS 13:48)

IT'S A NATURAL FACT:

ONLY FEMALE MOSQUITOES BITE!

BIBLE QUIZ:

WHO DID DAVID SAY THE LORD WOULD LAUGH AT?

THE WICKED (PSALM 37:12-13)

ANSWER TO "WHO AM I?" — DIETRICH BONHOEFFER

95

AWESOME TRUTH
by Eddie Eddings

"THERE ARE **TWO** KINDS OF PEOPLE: THOSE WHO SAY 'THY WILL BE DONE,' and THOSE TO WHOM GOD SAYS, 'ALL RIGHT, THEN, HAVE IT YOUR WAY.'"
— C.S. LEWIS

WHO AM I?

① BEFORE I WAS 13 I HAD A GOOD KNOWLEDGE OF LATIN, GREEK, AND HEBREW AND WAS WRITING PAPERS ON PHILOSOPHY.

② I PREACHED THE MOST FAMOUS SERMON IN AMERICAN HISTORY.

③ THREE OF MY BOOKS ARE: FREEDOM OF THE WILL, ORIGINAL SIN and RELIGIOUS AFFECTIONS.

(ANSWER BELOW)

IT WAS ABRAHAM LINCOLN WHO ESTABLISHED THANKSGIVING DAY AS AN ANNUAL HOLIDAY.

DALLAS, TEXAS WAS NAMED AFTER THE VICE-PRESIDENT OF THE U.S. IN 1845.

BIBLE QUIZ

NAME THE BOOK GIVEN TO JESUS TO READ IN THE SYNAGOGUE.

ISAIAH (LUKE 4:17)

MEDITATE ON THIS VERSE

"THE LORD HAS ESTABLISHED HIS THRONE IN THE HEAVENS; AND HIS SOVEREIGNTY RULES OVER ALL."

(PSALM 103:19) NASB

ANSWER TO "WHO AM I?" ———— JONATHAN EDWARDS

97

AWESOME TRUTH

by Eddie Eddings

"NOBODY EVER OUTGROWS SCRIPTURE; THE BOOK WIDENS AND DEEPENS WITH OUR YEARS."

C.H. SPURGEON

"IS IT NOT LAWFUL FOR ME TO DO WHAT I WILL WITH MINE OWN?"

MATTHEW 20:15

WHO AM I?

① MY FATHER AND I WERE BOTH PHARISEES.

② I WATCHED A GREAT CHRISTIAN DIE BY THE HANDS OF AN ANGRY MOB.

③ JESUS KNOCKED ME OFF MY HIGH HORSE WITH BLINDING LIGHT.

(ANSWER BELOW)

BIBLE QUIZ

NAME TWO MEN WHO FEARED A SMALL CHILD.

PHARAOH and HEROD
(EXODUS 1:22 + MATTHEW 2:3)

"DO WE HAVE A GOD WHO IS DESPERATELY TRYING TO SAVE EVERYBODY AND IS EQUALLY FAILING; OR DO WE HAVE A GOD WHO HAS SET HIS PURPOSE AND FIXED HIS HEART UPON HIS OWN PEOPLE, HIS ELECT, WHOM HE HATH CHOSEN BEFORE THE FOUNDATION OF THE WORLD? THE SOVEREIGN LORD GOD OF HEAVEN AND EARTH IS UNFAILINGLY BRINGING EVERYONE OF THEM INTO GLORY!"

D. JAMES KENNEDY

ANSWER TO "WHO AM I?" —— PAUL

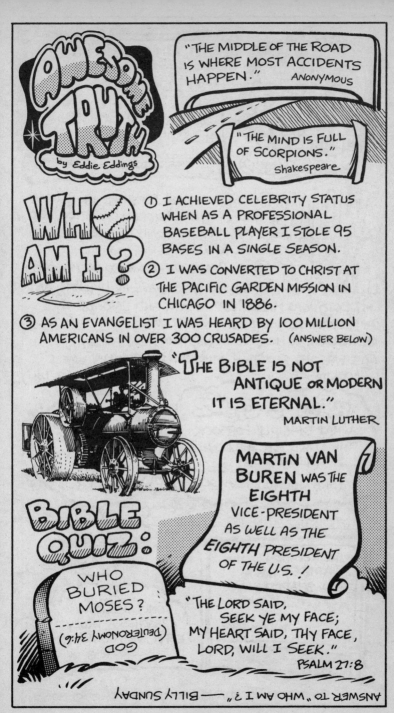

AWESOME TRUTH by Eddie Eddings

"THE MIDDLE OF THE ROAD IS WHERE MOST ACCIDENTS HAPPEN." ANONYMOUS

"THE MIND IS FULL OF SCORPIONS." Shakespeare

WHO AM I?

① I ACHIEVED CELEBRITY STATUS WHEN AS A PROFESSIONAL BASEBALL PLAYER I STOLE 95 BASES IN A SINGLE SEASON.

② I WAS CONVERTED TO CHRIST AT THE PACIFIC GARDEN MISSION IN CHICAGO IN 1886.

③ AS AN EVANGELIST I WAS HEARD BY 100 MILLION AMERICANS IN OVER 300 CRUSADES. (ANSWER BELOW)

"THE BIBLE IS NOT ANTIQUE OR MODERN IT IS ETERNAL." MARTIN LUTHER

MARTIN VAN BUREN WAS THE EIGHTH VICE-PRESIDENT AS WELL AS THE EIGHTH PRESIDENT OF THE U.S.!

BIBLE QUIZ:

WHO BURIED MOSES?

GOD (DEUTERONOMY 34:6)

"THE LORD SAID, SEEK YE MY FACE; MY HEART SAID, THY FACE, LORD, WILL I SEEK." PSALM 27:8

ANSWER TO "WHO AM I?" — BILLY SUNDAY

99

AWESOME TRUTH by Eddie Eddings

JAMES A. GARFIELD, 20th PRESIDENT OF THE U.S. COULD WRITE CLASSICAL GREEK WITH HIS LEFT HAND and CLASSICAL LATIN WITH HIS RIGHT SIMULTANEOUSLY!

WHO AM I?

① I SPENT OVER 30 YEARS IN AFRICA, MOSTLY IN UNEXPLORED COUNTRY, AND WAS THE ONE WHO DISCOVERED VICTORIA FALLS.

② MY HEART WAS REMOVED AND BURIED IN THE AFRICA I GAVE MY LIFE FOR, AND MY BODY WAS PRESERVED IN SALT AND CARRIED BY AFFECTIONATE NATIVES OVER 1,000 MILES AND ULTIMATELY BURIED WITH HONORS IN WESTMINSTER ABBEY.

③ I WAS THE SCOTTISH MISSIONARY STANLEY WAS LOOKING FOR.

(ANSWER BELOW)

BIBLE QUIZ

WHAT DISCIPLE FORSOOK THE LORD FOR THE LOVE OF THE WORLD?

DEMAS (2 TIMOTHY 4:10)

ARE YOU GIVING TO GOD WHAT IS RIGHT, OR WHAT IS LEFT?

"THE RELIGION OF THE ATHEIST HAS A GOD-SHAPED BLANK AT ITS HEART." H.G. Wells

"ONLY THE CALVINIST TEACHES A TRULY EFFECTIVE ATONEMENT." R.B. KUIPER

ANSWER TO "WHO AM I?" —— DAVID LIVINGSTONE

AWESOME TRUTH by Eddie Eddings

"MANY PRAY, 'LET THIS CUP PASS AWAY,' BUT FEW, 'THY WILL BE DONE.'"

— Thomas Watson

WHO AM I?

① I WAS THE PRINCIPAL TRANSLATOR OF THE GERMAN BIBLE BUT I ASKED FOR MY NAME NOT TO APPEAR IN THE PUBLICATION.

② AFTER 1521, I SPENT THE REST OF MY LIFE AN "OUTLAW."

③ I WROTE "A MIGHTY FORTRESS IS OUR GOD."

(ANSWER BELOW)

BIBLE QUIZ:

WHAT SIGNIFICANCE DO THESE NUMBERS HAVE IN CONNECTION WITH THE STUDY OF THE BIBLE:

66, 39, 27?

66 BOOKS IN THE BIBLE
39 IN THE OLD TESTAMENT
27 IN THE NEW TESTAMENT

AT THE AGE OF TEN, ABRAHAM LINCOLN HAD READ THE BIBLE THROUGH 3 TIMES!

THE CHURCH HAS MANY CRITICS BUT NO RIVALS!

BIBLE CHALLENGE:

TRY TO FIND A PASSAGE OR VERSE OF SCRIPTURE WHERE CHRISTIANS ARE TO PRAY THAT UNBELIEVERS WILL BE RECEPTIVE TO THE GOSPEL. — THERE ARE NONE! NOW TURN TO ISAIAH 55:11 and READ IT! WOW!

ANSWER TO "WHO AM I?" — MARTIN LUTHER

101

AWESOME TRUTH by Eddie Eddings

WHAT WE WEAVE IN TIME WE WEAR IN ETERNITY.

WHO AM I?

① I WAS AN ORPHAN THAT GOD USED TO PREVENT A HOLOCAUST IN THE OLD TESTAMENT.

② I WAS A BEAUTIFUL QUEEN WHO INTERCEDED FOR GOD'S CHOSEN PEOPLE.

③ MY DRAMA REACHED ITS CLIMAX IN A GRIPPING SCENE OF ULTIMATE POETIC JUSTICE. (ANSWER BELOW)

WASHINGTON IRVING, AUTHOR OF "RIP VAN WINKLE" and "LEGEND OF SLEEPY HOLLOW" WAS APPOINTED AMERICAN AMBASSADOR TO SPAIN IN 1842.

THE WORLDS LAST DODO BIRD DIED IN 1681. THE SAME YEAR THAT JOHN BUNYAN PUBLISHED "THE PILGRIM'S PROGRESS."

DON'T THINK I'LL HAVE TIME TO FINISH THIS ONE...

PILGRIMS PROGRESS

BIBLE QUIZ: WHO DIED WHILE WITNESSING? STEPHEN (ACTS 7:59)

ANSWER TO "WHO AM I?" — ESTHER

102

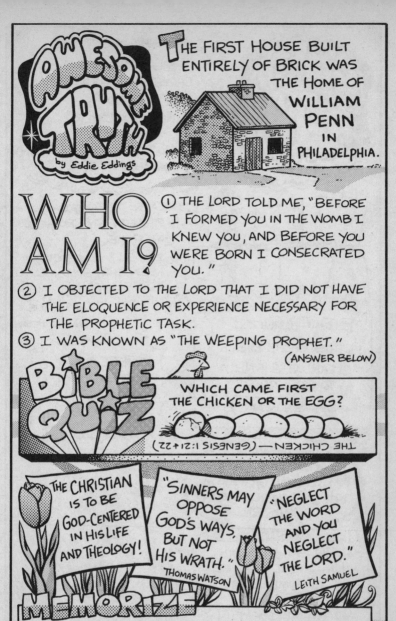

AWESOME TRUTH
by Eddie Eddings

THE FIRST HOUSE BUILT ENTIRELY OF BRICK WAS THE HOME OF WILLIAM PENN IN PHILADELPHIA.

WHO AM I?

① THE LORD TOLD ME, "BEFORE I FORMED YOU IN THE WOMB I KNEW YOU, AND BEFORE YOU WERE BORN I CONSECRATED YOU."

② I OBJECTED TO THE LORD THAT I DID NOT HAVE THE ELOQUENCE OR EXPERIENCE NECESSARY FOR THE PROPHETIC TASK.

③ I WAS KNOWN AS "THE WEEPING PROPHET."

(ANSWER BELOW)

BIBLE QUIZ

WHICH CAME FIRST THE CHICKEN OR THE EGG?

THE CHICKEN — (GENESIS 1:21 + 22)

THE CHRISTIAN IS TO BE GOD-CENTERED IN HIS LIFE AND THEOLOGY!

"SINNERS MAY OPPOSE GOD'S WAYS, BUT NOT HIS WRATH."
THOMAS WATSON

"NEGLECT THE WORD AND YOU NEGLECT THE LORD."
LEITH SAMUEL

MEMORIZE

"BLESSED BE THE LORD GOD OF ISRAEL, FOR HE HAS VISITED US AND ACCOMPLISHED REDEMPTION FOR HIS PEOPLE." —— LUKE 1:68

ANSWER TO "WHO AM I?" —— JEREMIAH

103

AWESOME TRUTH by Eddie Eddings

THE LAST **WORDS** OF CHRISTOPHER COLUMBUS (1451-1506), ITALIAN EXPLORER WERE "INTO THY HANDS, O LORD, I COMMEND MY SPIRIT."

WHO AM I?

① BECAUSE OF PATERNAL PARTIALITY, MY BROTHERS HATED ME.
② I WAS 17 YEARS OLD WHEN THEY SOLD ME INTO SLAVERY.
③ MY DREAMS CAME TRUE.
(ANSWER BELOW)

BIBLE QUIZ:
IS THIS IN THE BIBLE?
"CLEANLINESS IS NEXT TO GODLINESS."
NO (JOHN WESLEY SAID IT)

"WHERE CHRIST DOES NOT RULE, SIN DOES."
J.I. PACKER

THE GRAHAM CRACKER WAS INVENTED BY SYLVESTER GRAHAM, A 19th CENTURY NEW ENGLAND MINISTER.

"THIS IS THE MAN TO WHOM I WILL LOOK, HE THAT IS HUMBLE AND CONTRITE IN SPIRIT, AND TREMBLES AT MY WORD."
ISAIAH 66:2

ANSWER TO "WHO AM I?" ——— JOSEPH

104

AWESOME TRUTH

by Eddie Eddings

"MEN MAY HAVE ATHEISTICAL HEARTS WITHOUT ATHEISTICAL HEADS."

Stephen Charnock

WHO AM I?

① THE ELEMENTS OBEYED MY COMMANDS.

② MY PRAYERS WERE **ALWAYS** ANSWERED SPECIFICALLY.

③ I WAS BORN FOR THE PURPOSE OF **DYING**.

(ANSWER BELOW)

IT'S A FACT!

CHILDREN HAVE ALMOST **50% MORE BONES** THAN ADULTS. AN ADULT HAS 206 BONES; A CHILD HAS 300.

THE TEETH MAY BE FALSE, BUT LET THE TONGUE BE TRUE!

BIBLE QUIZ:

WHO WAS "WITHOUT A BLEMISH" IN THE OLD TESTAMENT?

2 SAMUEL 14:25
ABSALOM

THE **1st** INDIAN PREACHER OF CHRISTIANITY WAS **HIACOOMES**. THOMAS MAYHEW TAUGHT HIM TO READ AND WRITE. HE WAS ORDAINED AUGUST 22, 1670, BY JOHN COTTON and JOHN ELIOT.

THE MONA LISA IS PAINTED ON WOOD.

B.H. CARROLL (1843–1914) WAS THE FOUNDER OF SOUTHWESTERN BAPTIST SEMINARY AND A MEMBER OF THE TEXAS RANGERS!

ANSWER TO "WHO AM I?" ——— JESUS CHRIST

105

AWESOME TRUTH
by Eddie Eddings

"UNTIL WE HAVE COME TO THE PLACE WHERE WE CAN SING ABOUT ELECTION WITH A FULL HEART WE HAVE NOT GRASPED THE SPIRIT OF THE NEW TESTAMENT TEACHING."
— SINCLAIR FERGUSON

WHO AM I?

① I WAS THE LAST MAJOR THINKER OF THE ANCIENT WORLD AND THE FIRST PHILOSOPHER AND THEOLOGIAN OF THE MIDDLE AGES.

② BEFORE MY CONVERSION I LIVED A VERY IMMORAL LIFE. I FATHERED AN ILLEGITIMATE SON BEFORE I WAS TWENTY.

③ I BEGAN WRITING "THE CITY OF GOD" IN 413 A.D.

(ANSWER BELOW)

IT'S A LITTLE KNOWN FACT!

ALEXANDER GRAHAM BELL'S ASSISTANT — WATSON — WHO WAS THE FIRST TO RECIEVE A PHONE MESSAGE — "MR. WATSON, COME HERE, I WANT YOU " — WAS THE INVENTOR OF THE TELEPHONE BOOTH!

THE **ONLY** TWO WORDS THAT END WITH "GRY" ARE "ANGRY" AND "HUNGRY."

"THE BIBLE IS A WINDOW IN THIS PRISON OF HOPE, THROUGH WHICH WE LOOK INTO ETERNITY." — DWIGHT

ANSWER TO "WHO AM I ?" — AUGUSTINE OF HIPPO

AWESOME TRUTH by Eddie Eddings

"YOU WILL BE A BELIEVER SOMEDAY. IF YOU NEVER BELIEVE ON EARTH, YOU WILL BELIEVE IN HELL."

— BROWNLOW NORTH

WHO AM I?

① THROUGH THE INFLUENCE OF MY SUNDAY SCHOOL TEACHER, EDWARD KIMBALL, I WAS CONVERTED TO CHRIST.

② AT ONE TIME I WAS A TRAVELING SALESMAN BUT GAVE UP THE BUSINESS TO SPEND MY FULL TIME IN SUNDAY SCHOOL AND YMCA WORK.

③ I ENLISTED IRA SANKEY AS MY MUSICAL ASSOCIATE FOR MY EVANGELISTIC CAMPAIGNS. (ANSWER BELOW)

THE KOALA EATS ONLY THE LEAVES OF THE EUCALYPTUS TREES — and ONLY ON THE LEAVES OF 5 OUT OF THE 350 SPECIES OF EUCALYPTUS AT THAT!

BIBLE QUIZ:

WHO DIED FOR DENOUNCING HEROD?

(JOHN THE BAPTIST) (MARK 6:18-28)

"A MAN CANNOT BE THOROUGHLY HUMBLED UNTIL HE COMES TO KNOW THAT HIS SALVATION IS UTTERLY BEYOND HIS OWN POWERS, COUNSEL, ENDEAVOURS, WILL, AND WORKS, AND IS ABSOLUTELY DEPENDENT UPON THE WILL, COUNSEL AND PLEASURE OF ANOTHER." — MARTIN LUTHER

ANSWER TO "WHO AM I?" — D.L. MOODY

AWESOME TRUTH
by Eddie Eddings

"WE MUST BELIEVE IN THE GRACE OF SOVEREIGNTY AS WELL AS THE SOVEREIGNTY OF GRACE."

AUGUSTUS H. STRONG

WHO AM I?

① BECAUSE OF A PERMANENT MISFOCUS OF MY EYES I WAS REFERRED TO AMONG THE RIFF-RAFF OF LONDON AS "DOCTOR SQUINTUM."

② I WAS THE FIRST "CALVINIST-METHODIST," YET I LIVED AND DIED A PRIEST OF THE CHURCH OF ENGLAND.

③ I WAS THE CHIEF FIGURE OF THE GREAT AWAKENING IN AMERICA.

(ANSWER BELOW)

BIBLE QUIZ

WHO HAD 12 FINGERS and 12 TOES IN THE OLD TESTAMENT?

(A GIANT AT GATH (2 SAMUEL 21:20-22)

"A CHRISTIAN IS THE WORLD'S BIBLE... AND SOME OF THEM NEED REVISING."

D.L. MOODY

"ELECTION IS NOT CHEAP... FOR EACH MAN CHOSEN BY GOD THERE IS A PRICE OF REDEMPTION. THAT PRICE IS SAID TO BE THE SPRINKLING OF THE BLOOD OF JESUS CHRIST."

——PAIGE PATTERSON

ANSWER TO "WHO AM I?" ———— GEORGE WHITEFIELD

108

AWESOME TRUTH

by Eddie Eddings

"WE BELIEVE THAT THE MOST SCIENTIFIC VIEW, THE MOST UP-TO-DATE AND RATIONALISTIC CONCEPTION, WILL FIND ITS FULLEST SATISFACTION IN TAKING THE BIBLE STORY LITERALLY."

WINSTON CHURCHILL

WHO AM I?

① AT 21 YEARS OF AGE I WAS ENGLAND'S NATIONAL CRICKETING HERO.

② IN 1875 I WAS CONVERTED TO CHRIST THROUGH D.L. MOODY AND BECAME WHAT I CALL... "A REAL LIVE PLAY-THE-GAME CHRISTIAN."

③ I ABANDONED FAME AND FORTUNE (I WAS BORN IN LUXURY) TO BECOME A MISSIONARY.

(ANSWER BELOW)

EVER HEARD THE FRENCH SONG "AH! VOUS DIRAIJE MAMAN," WRITTEN IN 1765? FROM THAT TUNE WE GET "THE ALPHABET SONG," "TWINKLE, TWINKLE LITTLE STAR," and "BAA, BAA, BLACK SHEEP." ALL HAVE THE SAME MELODY.

BIBLE QUIZ

WHAT BIBLE CHARACTER WAS THE FATHER OF **88 CHILDREN?**

(28 SONS and 60 DAUGHTERS)
REHOBOAM

THE WORLD'S FIRST CHRISTMAS CARD WAS CREATED IN ENGLAND IN 1843.

A COMPLETELY BLIND CHAMELEON WILL STILL TAKE ON THE COLORS OF ITS ENVIRONMENT!

ANSWER TO "WHO AM I?" —— C.T. STUDD

OWESOME TRUTH by Eddie Eddings

"CHRISTIANITY, IF FALSE, IS OF NO IMPORTANCE, AND, IF TRUE, OF INFINITE IMPORTANCE. THE ONE THING IT CANNOT BE IS MODERATELY IMPORTANT." — C.S. LEWIS

WHO AM I?

① I AM CALLED "THE FATHER OF THE ENGLISH BIBLE."

② I WAS BETRAYED BY A FELLOW ENGLISHMAN, CONFINED TO PRISON AND EVENTUALLY EXECUTED FOR TRANSLATING THE SCRIPTURES.

③ MY LAST WORDS WERE: "LORD, OPEN THE KING OF ENGLAND'S EYES." (ANSWER BELOW)

BIBLE QUIZ

WHAT BOOK RECORDS THE STORY OF BOAZ?

RUTH

THOMAS JEFFERSON INVENTED THE DUMB-WAITER and THE SWIVEL CHAIR!

"GOD LOVES TO SHOW MERCY. HE IS NOT HESITANT OR INDECISIVE OR TENTATIVE IN HIS DESIRES TO DO GOOD TO HIS PEOPLE. HIS ANGER MUST BE RELEASED BY A STIFF SAFETY LOCK BUT HIS MERCY HAS A HAIR TRIGGER." — JOHN PIPER

"THE LORD, THE LORD, A GOD MERCIFUL AND GRACIOUS, SLOW TO ANGER, AND ABOUNDING IN STEADFAST LOVE." (EXODUS 34:6)

ANSWER TO "WHO AM I?" — WILLIAM TYNDALE

AWESOME TRUTH
by Eddie Eddings

"NOTHING IS POLITICALLY RIGHT WHICH IS MORALLY WRONG."
— DANIEL O'CONNELL

WHO AM I?

1. I ABSOLUTELY HATED THE PEOPLE I PREACHED TO.
2. I WENT OVERBOARD WITH MY REBELLION.
3. I WAS HELD CAPTIVE BY MONSTEROUS CIRCUMSTANCES.

(ANSWER BELOW)

THE JOINING OF HANDS DURING PRAYER IS NOT MENTIONED IN THE BIBLE. IT BECAME PART OF THE CHRISTIAN TRADITION IN THE 9th CENTURY. UNTIL THAT TIME, THE MOST COMMON POSTURE OF PRAYER INVOLVED THE SPREADING OF ARMS AND HANDS TOWARD HEAVEN. CHRISTIANS ADOPTED THE GESTURE REPRESENTING THE SHACKLED HANDS OF A PRISONER AS A SIGN OF MAN'S TOTAL OBEDIENCE TO DIVINE POWER.

THE FIRST PRESIDENT TO BE BORN IN THE 20th CENTURY WAS JOHN F. KENNEDY.

READ THIS VERSE

AND TELL ME WHO "GUARDIAN ANGELS" GUARD ....

"ARE THEY NOT ALL MINISTERING SPIRITS, (REFERRING TO ANGELS IN PREVIOUS VERSE) SENT FORTH TO MINISTER FOR THEM WHO SHALL BE HEIRS OF SALVATION?"

HEBREWS 1:14

THERE ARE NO ENGLISH WORDS THAT RHYME WITH ORANGE, PURPLE OR SILVER

NONE AT ALL!

ANSWER TO "WHO AM I?" — JONAH

111

If you have any "Awesome Truth" you would like to see in the next volume, send it (with documentation, if possible) along with your name, address, and phone number. We'd also love to hear your comments about this edition of Awesome Truth.

Eddie Eddings
c/o Barbour & Company, Inc.
P.O. Box 719
Uhrichsville, OH 44683